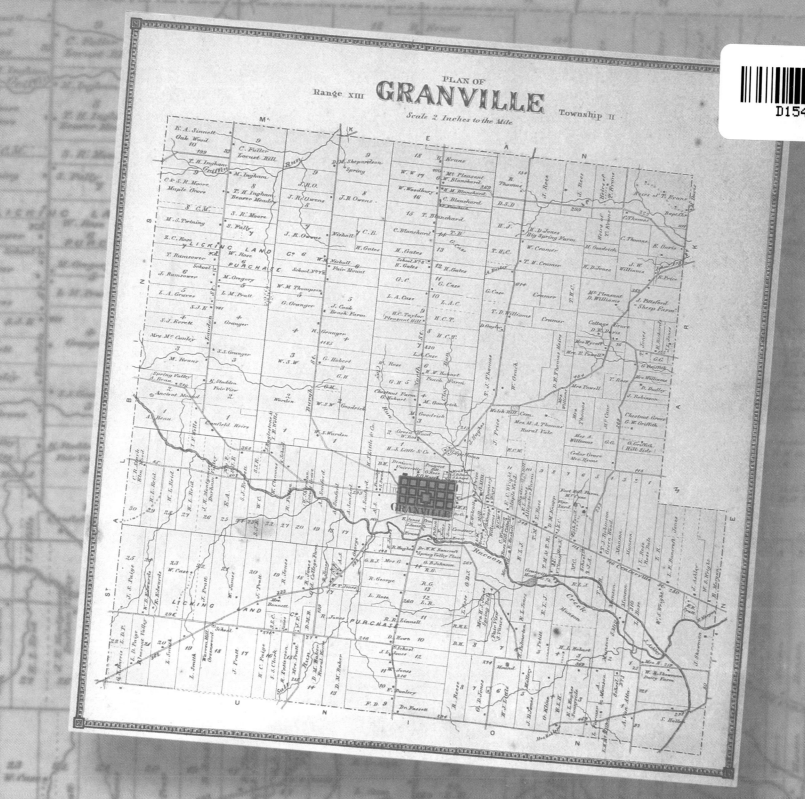

PLAN OF

GRANVILLE

Range XIII   Township II

Scale 2 Inches to the Mile

Images Past AND Present

Granville; looking south down Main Street from College Hill on a snowy day, about 1900.

GRANVILLE, OHIO
A Study in Continuity and Change

VOLUME III
Images Past
AND
Present

Edited by

THERESA S. OVERHOLSER
FLORENCE W. HOFFMAN

Wally Chessmans volume!

Granville Historical Society
Denison University Press
Granville, Ohio

Maps on the front endpaper are from the *Atlas of Licking Co. Ohio*, Beers, Soule & Co., 1866. Maps on the back endpaper are from the *Combination Atlas Map of Licking County, Ohio,* by L. H. Everts, 1875.

Additional copies may be obtained from:
Granville Historical Society
P. O. Box 129
Granville, Ohio 43023-0129
Phone: 740 587-3951
Email: office@granvillehistory.org
Website: www.granvillehistory.org

Book design and production by Fishergate, Inc.
www.fishergate.com

CONTENTS

This book is dedicated to
the Bills,
who made it possible.

INTRODUCTION

This book is a glimpse of Granville during its first 200 years. It touches on the change from nearly unbroken woodland to a suburban environment. We are indebted to the 1805 pioneers who organized the Licking Company to buy land and settle in the "West." They laid out a regular grid for streets in their new town, oriented to the compass points. They determined that the Broad Way should be ten rods wide (165 ft.) and Main Street six rods (99 ft.) They established schools, churches, and a stable democratic government and determined the look and feel of the environment we see today, as we have chronicled in this volume.

Building on this strong foundation, their successors embraced new ideas and technological improvements. Entrepreneurs seized business and professional opportunities. Commitment to education also encouraged interest in literature, music, and the arts, which became integral to community life. Granville citizens discussed, differed, supported each other, and seldom missed the chance to come together in celebration. As the years passed, the need to preserve the records of past events led to family, church, and historical collections, all of which have provided resources for this work. It is our hope that this volume will be interesting and accessible to the general reader while providing richer detail to those already familiar with Granville's history.

—THERESA S. OVERHOLSER
FLORENCE W. HOFFMAN
Editors

Granville, Ohio, July 2004

CHAPTER 1

Granville, Ohio
on the eve of its 200th birthday

(Both images)
Granville Historical Society Archives

1

Directions to any Granville location
begin, "Come to the four churches corner and . . ."

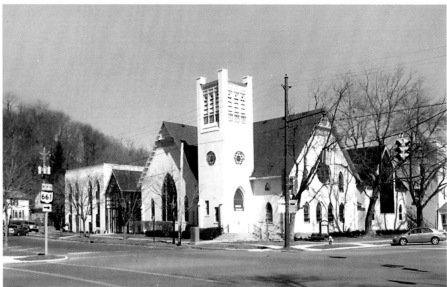

(All four images)
Granville Historical Society Archives

The lively downtown scene.
Granville Historical Society Archives

A cool drink on a warm day
at the Broadway Fountain.
The Granville Sentinel

Summer Saturday at the Farmer's Market.
The Granville Sentinel

Granville cherishes its historic heritage

The front section of the Elias Gilman House was built in 1808 and is the oldest dwelling in Granville. The house is now owned by the Kappa Alpha Theta Sorority.

The Avery-Downer House on East Broadway is an outstanding example of Greek Revival architecture.

(Above and top)
Granville Historical Society Archives

Laura Cramer portrays one of the pioneers buried in the Old Colony Burying Ground during an annual tour of the cemetery.

The Granville Sentinel
Photo: Charles A. Peterson

Students from the Elementary School display
the state banner awarded for school excellence.

Granville enjoys the four seasons

Summer: High School reunions and the Fourth of July—Allan Ellis, Class of 1936, aboard a float in the Independence Day parade.

The Granville Sentinel
Photo: Charles A. Peterson

Spring: Jim Siegel and spring blossoms in Opera House Park.

The Granville Sentinel

Autumn: Dick Mahard at the dedication of the Ohio Historic Marker for the Old Academy Building.

Granville Historical Society Archives

Winter: Walking the dog beside the Denison Fine Arts Campus on West Broadway.

The Granville Sentinel
Photo: Charles A. Peterson

Granville remembers its past and looks to the future

American Legion Commander Edith Jobe with Paul Jobe at the Memorial Day Services at Maple Grove Cemetery in 1998.

(Both images)
The Granville Sentinel

Memorial Day in Granville.

"Granville township is a tract of choice land five miles square, centrally located in the county of Licking, State of Ohio. Through the center of it, from west to east, runs the middle fork of the Pataskala, or Licking River, this branch being commonly called Raccoon Creek. Irregularly skirting the stream on either hand is a chain of hills from one to two hundred feet high, out of whose tops excellent stone is quarried, and from whose base flow perennial springs. They are diversified with ridges, knobs, spurs, and buttes, and here and there the chain is broken by the valleys through which the brooks, fed by those springs, find their way into the leading stream. This is the locality, the events of which are narrated in the following chapters."

—Henry Bushnell, *The History of Granville*

Denison University Archives

CHAPTER 2

The Setting:
A Granville Geography

Geography, it has been said, is the inescapable setting of history. It includes such elements as climate, land forms, drainage, water courses, weather, soil, and vegetation. Early Welsh and Yankee settlers of the Granville area set out to purchase tracts of land large enough for their purposes, in both cases sending out "scouts" to look over the territory before the main settlement was established. The reports of the scouts were favorable. The particular geography of Granville had produced a most pleasant location for habitation, situated in the rolling hills of the Appalachian plateau, well-watered by springs and creeks, with good soil created by glaciation and weathering. And for a town site, there was a south-facing terrace above Raccoon Creek, sheltered on three sides by hills, but open to the sun. The surrounding forested hills produced wood and stone for building. There was plenty of gently rolling land for farming. A good living would be possible there. Based on these reports, the migrations began.

"One may pinpoint Granville on the face of the globe with almost absurd accuracy. At the point where the Lancaster road passes the depot at the foot of the hill, the Longitude is W. 82° 31' . . . At this [bike path] crossing the Latitude is N. 40° 03' 51.7". . . . at this same crossing one is 910.5 feet above the sea. The Administration Building on top of College Hill has a reading at its base of 1082.33 feet."

—William T. Utter, *Granville: The Story of an Ohio Village*

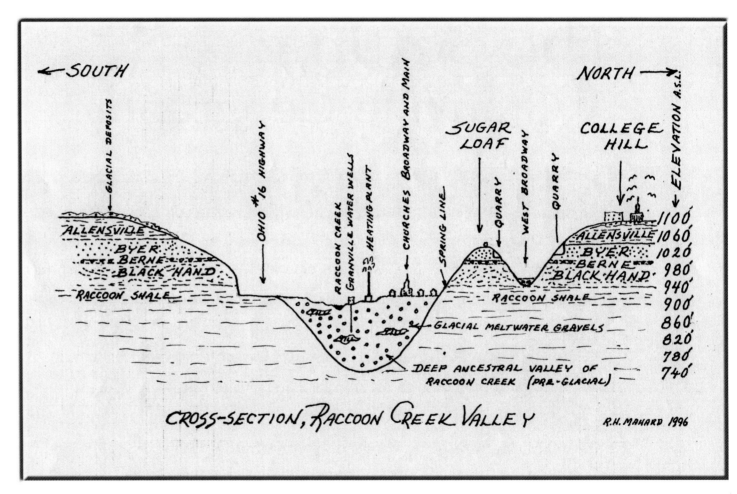

A drawing of the underlying geology of Granville, drawn and used by Professor Richard Mahard at Denison University.

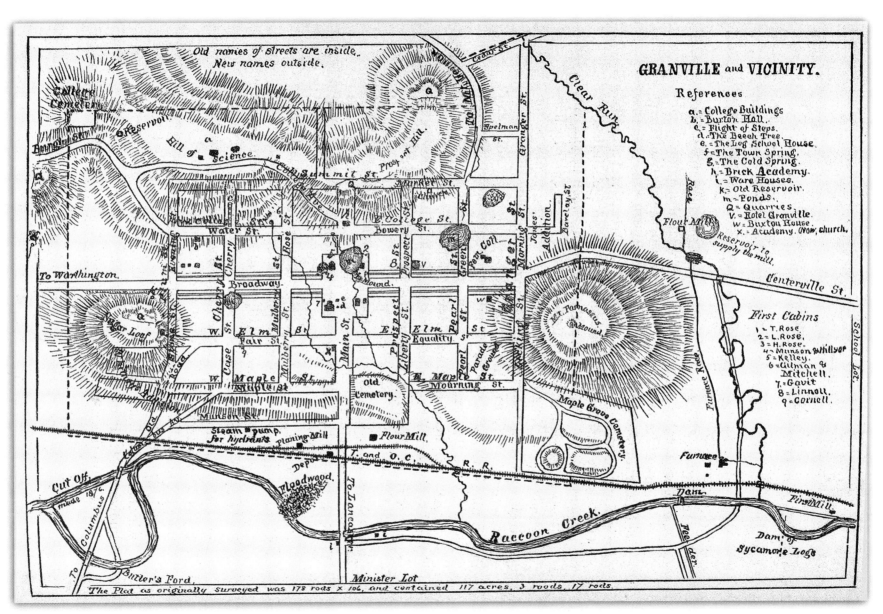

This interesting map appeared in *The History of Granville* by Henry Bushnell, published in 1889.

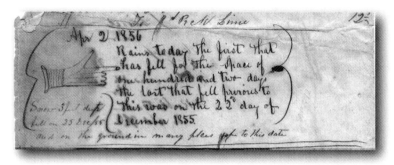

The weather in Granville is almost never "normal," as this 1856 chronicle demonstrates. The faint writing at the lower left says: "snow 3 feet deep fell on 25 Dec/55 and on the ground in many places to this date."

An ice storm transfigures the everyday intersection of North Pearl and College.

Raccoon Creek in one of its periodic floods. The view is of the old Columbus Road bridge, near today's water treatment plant.

A crowd of men and boys gathers at the South Pearl and Broadway corner to watch the clean-up after a summer storm, 1920s.

A new tree sprouts in the forest. Granville has grown increasingly shady as its trees grow larger and its surrounding hills are no longer used for the harvesting of hardwood.

(All images on this page and facing page)
Granville Historical Society Archives

This sheltered spring, located just east of 540 West Broadway, was known as Wilson's Spring or Collins' Spring. It was covered up in the 1970s when a set of brick condominiums was built on the property.

Clear Run, the creek that flows under Welsh Hills Road, through the Granville Golf Course, and under Newark Road, was important economically to the first residents as they used its waters in manufacturing and milling.

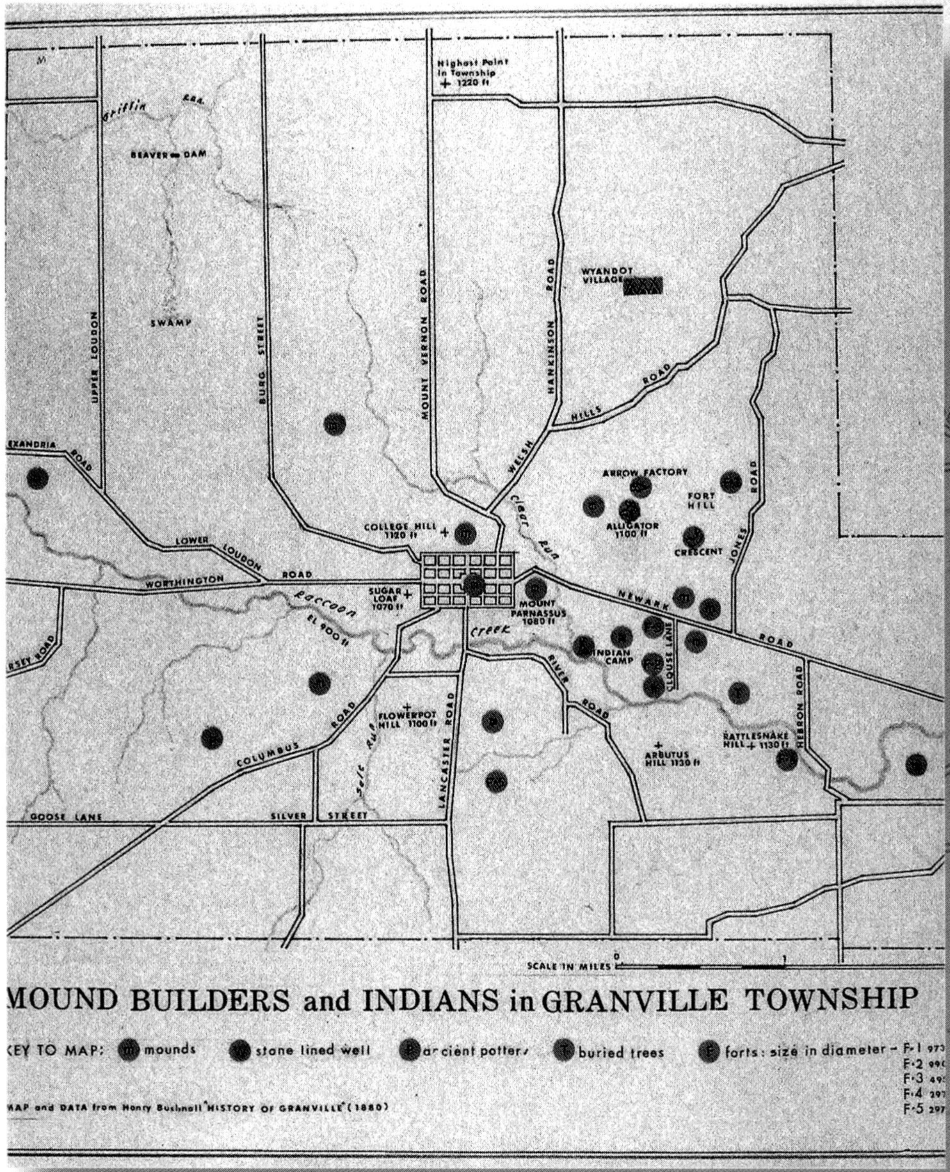

MOUND BUILDERS and INDIANS in GRANVILLE TOWNSHIP

KEY TO MAP: ⓜ mounds ● stone lined well ● ancient pottery Ⓣ buried trees Ⓕ forts: size in diameter - F-1 973

F-2 990
F-3 49⊘
F-4 297
F-5 297

MAP and DATA from Henry Bushnell "HISTORY of GRANVILLE" (1880)

The first historic settlers discovered that others had found the Raccoon valley to their liking. The evidence was present throughout the township, with a concentration just to the east of the village, and extending to the great earthworks in Newark.

The Lone Tree, a specimen of sour gum, *Nyssa Sylvatica*, measured 109 feet to its lowest branch. In comparison, some modern cellular phone towers are 170 feet tall. The giant was hit by lightning nearly every summer, until it finally burned and fell in 1923.

"I went up the hill that overhangs the village, on which stands the University, and resting under some trees enjoyed the scene. I looked down upon . . . a rolling landscape of gentle hills, with here and there golden wheat-fields in a setting of livid green—there were farms, forests, and sentinel trees upon the slopes and in the meadows of the valley, while over all was the tender blue sky and floating cumulus snowy-white clouds to flit their shadows."

—Henry Howe in *Howe's Historical Collections of Ohio*

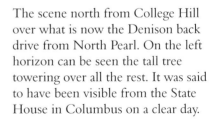

The scene north from College Hill over what is now the Denison back drive from North Pearl. On the left horizon can be seen the tall tree towering over all the rest. It was said to have been visible from the State House in Columbus on a clear day.

(Images on this page and facing page)
Granville Historical Society Archives

On a winter day in 1890 a local photographer climbed to the summit of Sugar Loaf Hill and shot the following cycloramic set of pictures. They offer a fascinating moment-in-time experience of Granville, and an interesting look at its surrounding geography.

Looking east toward Mt. Parnassus, West Elm at lower right. Dr. Edwin Sinnett's home appears on the barren hilltop.

The view has shifted just a little bit toward the south. The Old Colony Burying Ground is plainly visible at the right center.

The Old Colony slips out of the left side of the picture, as the camera points southeast.

Looking south-southeast toward Maple Street. The engine puffs along what has become the T. J. Evans bike path, with Raccoon Creek shining in the background.

This series of twelve pictures continues on the next four pages . . .

(All twelve images, unless otherwise noted)
Granville Historical Society Archives

The view to the south.

Raccoon Creek valley showing the location of the old Columbus Road and bridge. The corn field in the right foreground is the location of the village water treatment plant. Salt Run in the upper center winds its way through Spring Valley.

The site of the Granville Square Apartments, Wildwood Park, and, in the distance, Route 37.

Denison University Archives

Looking west toward Thorne's Hill. The rectangular field just beyond the last house on Broadway is now Wildwood Drive.

The area where Thresher Street meets Broadway. The five-unit apartment building was known as Kylesville and was a great wonder to residents of the village. The houses on the hill are on Burg Street.

A view of Denison University on the hill and the campus of Shepardson College for Women on West Broadway.

The Gilpatrick (right) and Colwell (left) residences on College Hill.

Looking back at bare Sugar Loaf from Thorne's Hill on the same day. Note the white horse grazing in the left foreground; the same horse is barely visible near Broadway in the photo looking at Thorne's Hill from the east.

Granville meets geology. In the autumn of 1900 one Ed Tight conceived the idea of using a large boulder as a family monument in Maple Grove Cemetery. A suitable rock, transported to the area thousands of years ago by a glacier, was found in a ravine west of town. Plans were made by Ed and his friend George Richards to retrieve it. A derrick was taken to the site to raise the ten or eleven ton granite boulder some 500 feet to level land. Twenty pairs of oxen and horses pulled it to the hard road, where two steam tractors took over. Ed constructed a special wagon for the five-mile trip to town. The wagon had wheels of solid wood, fifteen inches thick, with iron hubs and six-inch steel axles. It was necessary to brace several bridges on the route. At the cemetery, a special hoist was used so that one man, using one hand, could raise or lower the rock to place it in its setting, where it can be seen today.

(Both images)
Granville Historical Society Archives

The limits of the Village of Granville in 2004.

Granville Village Planning Department

Haying time on the Richards farm on North Street. By the 1920s,
when this picture was taken, machinery had been in use for many
decades, and fields were cleared from fenceline to fenceline.

The William T. Richards Family, courtesy of Patricia Battiston

CHAPTER 3

The Bountiful Land

Imagine arriving in what is now Granville Township in 1802 or in 1805 after weeks of hard travel, your family, a few goods, and a couple of cows in tow. It is, in the year of 1805, nearly winter. There is "nothing" but the vast beech-maple forest, a few small streams, and a clearing or two. What will you do to shelter and feed and clothe your family? The hardy Welsh and Yankee families of Granville had the skills and knowledge to solve this problem. They also had come to a most bountiful land which offered raw materials, wild animals and fish, and fruits and nuts from the forest until fields could be cleared and planted. These pioneers and the next generations of farmers labored to produce what they needed for themselves and for trade in the Eastern markets. The fruitful land bloomed in response to their labors.

By the late nineteenth century, machines were allowing more acres to be planted and harvested and more products to be shipped. Herds could be improved with well-bred animals delivered via the railroad. Inventors turned their ingenuity to making implements that eased toil. Households with small lots enjoyed fresh eggs and fruits and vegetables in season from their own backyards.

Two hundred years after the first settlements, once-productive fields are becoming roads and new homes. A few working farms remain in the Township, although nearby areas could still be considered rural. In the Village, many backyards sport large home additions, garages, or landscaped terraces and ponds where vegetable gardens once flourished. And many old farm fields have grown up to trees once again.

The Granville Sentinel

As the settlers went about organizing their lives and livelihoods, they established their herds of animals. Because clearing and fencing fields was a task that took several seasons, the animals often roamed or strayed. The farmers resorted to an ancient method of identifying their property: the earmark. Earmarks were combinations of slits and shapes cut into the animals' ears, each farmer having his own set which he used on "cattle sheep and swine." Pictured is the first page of the ear mark registry of Granville Township, dating from 1807.

Granville Historical Society Archives

(All three images:)
Granville Historical Society Archives

Augustine Munson, 1783-1868, brigadier general in the militia, member of the Ohio legislature.

One source of income for the earliest settlers was the trapping of fur-bearing wildlife. Augustine Munson, whose name is on this receipt, was one of the youngest land-owners in the settlement in 1806. He and his father, Jesse, owned many acres north and south of Newark-Granville Road, including Raccoon Creek bottom land, where raccoons and muskrats would have been plentiful.

RESIDENCE OF THE LATE GENERAL MUNSON. LOTS 1 AND 2 GRANVILLE TP. LICKING COUNTY OHIO. BUILT IN THE YEAR 1810.

This drawing from the 1875 Atlas of Licking County shows the farmhouse of Jesse and Augustine Munson, on the north side of Newark-Granville Road, east of Jones Road. The house was moved east and to the opposite side of the road to become the core of the Welsh Hills School in 1992. (See page 85.)

"Pork is the all absorbing question with us here at present. We butchered on Wednesday 17 hogs average 272 lbs. Pa intends killing his 50 on Tuesday. A roaring days work it will be for men and women."

—Letter from Deborah Devinney to her sister Anne Sheldon, Winter 1838

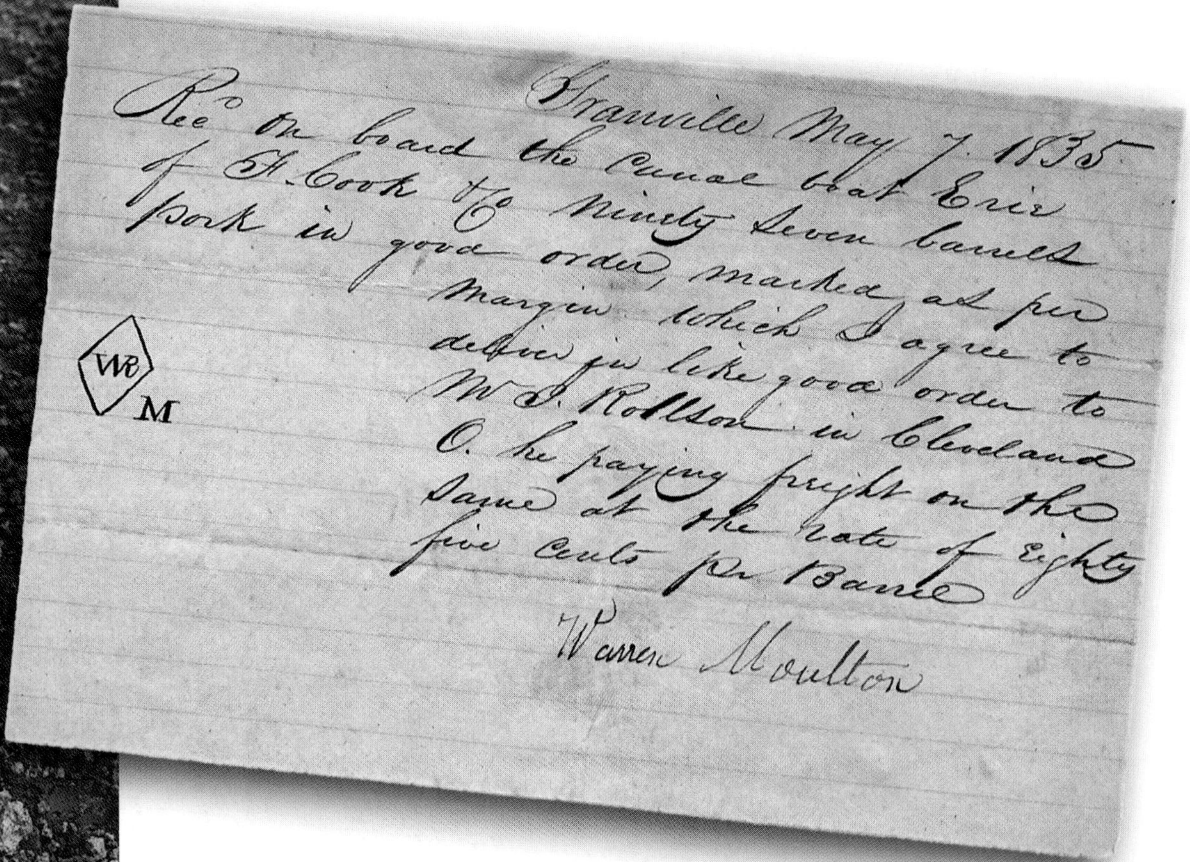

Granville Life-Style Museum

After hogs were butchered, the meat was smoked to become the family's winter protein. In the mid 1830s, excess was shipped via canal north to Cleveland, as this receipt shows. Lard was also exported in this way.

Granville Historical Society Archives

Leisha Hurwitz

Ellen Hayes' childhood memories of Granville in the 1850s are vividly written in her book *Wild Turkeys and Tallow Candles*. In the quotations from the book used with the pictures on this page and the next page, she describes her Grandfather Wolcott's farm at the northeastern foot of Mt. Parnassus and the agricultural fair held in Newark in what is now Moundbuilders Park.

"The farm was fenced, in part at least, with rails split from black walnut trees grown on the acres thus enclosed." [The rails pictured here enclose a farm on Lancaster Road, but would have been similar to the ones the Wolcotts used.]

(Both images:)
Granville Historical Society Archives

"One of the chief assets of this farm was the deep-seated never-failing spring at the foot of the hill and near the road—also not far from the kitchen door. . . it was sheltered by an ample brick spring-house around which grew various trees, mostly poplars. Stones had been placed so as to form a brim for the water which welled up from a sandy bottom and flowed leisurely out over a spread of pebbles and found exit from the spring-house on the side toward the road. In all weathers except the coldest, grandmother set her crocks of milk and cream in the shallow running water, and often the churning was done in the spring-house or in the shade just outside the door."

"How very distracting to have to see so much in one short day! We made the rounds of the stock exhibit where many pieces of scantling had been freshly and wantonly jabbed into those ancient artificial slopes to build pens for sheep and hogs, horses and cattle. We went up and down through the 'fine arts' building, the poultry houses, the horticultural hall. Ducks and calves and squashes and cut flowers, embroidery and jellies and ears of corn—the prides of many homesteads— were here displayed, each owner intent on winning a blue ribbon. I had believed that my own dear ducks were the finest ever; and now I saw that they were not."

(Both images:)
Granville Historical Society Archives

View of the Ohio State Fair grounds (showing the ancient embankment,) at Newark, 1854. The stalls occupy a circle, outside of the embankment, and the halls, tents, horse and cattle rings, the inner area.

The Licking County Agricultural Society gave elaborate certificates as awards at the county fair. Fanciful illustrations of farmers and their bounty bordered the recipient's and the prize-winning animal's names. This document was given to George Hagerty in 1866 for a thoroughbred bull called "Trogan."

Shorthorn cattle were first raised in Granville by Augustine Munson in the 1830s. At the end of the nineteenth century there were several large farms in and near the township which specialized in breeding stock. One of these was the establishment of John Montgomery on the Worthington Road. His farm is the Raccoon International Golf Club in 2004. Notice the explicit instructions for reaching Granville by rail.

Granville Historical Society Archives

CATALOGUE

OF THE

DURHAM VALLEY HERD

OF

Short Horn Cattle,

BELONGING TO

JOHN H. MONTGOMERY,

GRANVILLE, LICKING COUNTY, OHIO.

JULY, 1879.

DURHAM VALLEY FARM is 25 miles east of Columbus, 8 miles west of Newark, and 2 miles west of Granville. Daily Bus from Newark to Granville. Hack for every train from Union Station to Granville, which is 3 miles south of Granville, on the B. & O. and P. C. & St. L. R'ys. The two Railroads connect at Columbus and Newark, both running on the same track from the two last places mentioned.

COLUMBUS, OHIO:
GAZETTE STEAM PRINTING HOUSE.
1879.

This newspaper photograph from 1968 shows the auctioneer and a soon to be sold cow. The building burned in the 1980s.

The Newark Advocate

These two steers belonged to the Devinney family who farmed on Loudon Street just north of the township line. A newspaper article of December, 1890 called them "two of the finest short-horn cattle ever raised in this county. The two together weighed 4,090 pounds and were perfect beauties." The animals are pictured, on the first part of their trip to a buyer in Boston, in front of 590 West Broadway, the home of Emma Devinney Robinson.

Granville Life-Style Museum

For several decades weekly livestock auctions took place in a ramshackle series of buildings on Munson Street.

The Granville Sentinel

In the second half of the nineteenth century family farms and the homes on them were often sources of great pride. Photographers and engravers traveled the county making pictures of families, buildings, and animals. The properties were given names such as "Fair Mount," and "Locust Grove," and, especially meaningful to Granville, "Alligator Farm."

RES. OF ABNER BEAN. GRANVILLE TP. LICKING CO. OHIO.

The farm of Abner Bean was pictured in the 1875 *Atlas of Licking County*. The home stands in 2004 at 3708 Raccoon Valley Road.

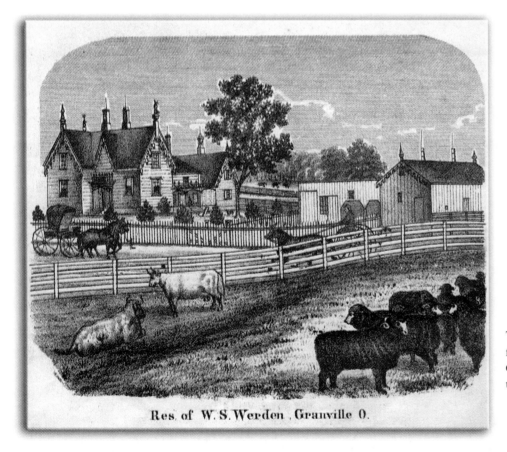

Res. of W. S. Werden, Granville O.

The Werden Farm, shown here from the 1866 *Atlas of Licking County*, was on Burg Street near the Chelsea Drive intersection.

(All images on this page and facing page)
Granville Historical Society Archives

Spring Valley Place was on Lancaster Road just south of Raccoon Creek, on the east side of the road. This picture is from the 1866 *Atlas of Licking County*.

The Williams family poses outside their home at 2500 Raccoon Valley Road.

"SPRING VALLEY PLACE"
Res. of Dr W. W. Bancroft, Granville O.

Spring Valley Place was later purchased by the Wilson family, who were the owners when this photograph was taken. The house was moved and now stands at 935 River Road where it is used by a variety of businesses.

(All six images:)
The William T. Richards Family, courtesy of Patricia Battiston

The threshing of grain, the mechanical separating of the seeds, was a time of great excitement and exhausting labor on the farm. Usually one man in the neighborhood owned a threshing machine which he and a team of workers would haul around to other farms in turn. The host family provided a huge noontime meal for all involved, the best and most food that could be prepared. In this early 1900s photograph men are feeding cut stalks into the Peerless thresher, which, in a series of processes, shakes out the seeds and blows the straw into a pile.

Two types of horse power are at the ready on the Richards farm on North Street in 1931. The tractor is pulling a disc harrow, which pulverized the soil in preparation for planting. The horses are hitched to a seed planting implement.

Harvesting on the same farm, also in 1931.

A clover huller was a different type of thresher which was designed to separate the very fine clover seeds from the plant stems.

A newer threshing machine in use from 1924 to 1938. The steam tractor powered farm machinery by means of belts and wheels.

A barn-building in 1912. This large undertaking was supervised by Hubert Robinson and Wat Thomas on property belonging to Robinson's father on Columbus Road near Goose Lane.

Granville Life-Style Museum

By 1919 area farmers had changed their opinion of the Grange movement. A local chapter was formed with Wilkin T. Jones as Master. In the early winter of 1922-1923 the group purchased the Old Academy Building at Main and Elm Streets from the Welsh Congregational Church. This photograph of Grange members was taken in 1948.

Granville Historical Society Archives

In 1854 a group of farmers from what is now Newark-Granville Road formed an organization for education and mutual support. They called themselves the Centerville Farmers Club, Centerville Street being the old name for the road. A few years later the name became the Granville Farmers Club, as membership expanded to other areas of the township. At each monthly meeting the topic of discussion for the next session was announced, and members were to prepare any remarks on the subject. Among the discussions were such things as diseases of sheep, compulsory education, farm field fertility, hedge growing, the game laws of Ohio. In 1873, one of the topics was the Farmer's Grange Movement. Members of the club were for the most part unimpressed by the movement, which was designed to improve the condition of the farmer through education and cooperative buying and marketing. The consensus was that the Grange did little more than Granville farmers could do on their own.

The 1850 U.S. Census of Agriculture shows a total of 153 farms in Granville Township, ranging in size from eight acres to over 400, with more than half being 100 or fewer acres. In the 1870 census, the number of farms was 151. Clearly, Granville was a rural community, and one did not go far outside the original village boundaries before coming to farmland.

Dr. Sinnett's lands were taken over by the doctor's son-in-law, Charles Browne White, who grew peaches in the hilltop orchard. Those same hilltop lands had been used for an apple orchard by Horace Wolcott, Ellen Hayes' grandfather.

The Granville Times

The large building to the left of center was the Union School, on the Granger Street site of today's Elementary building. The shocked grain is in a field belonging to Dr. Edwin Sinnett; the location is now the Granville Golf Course.
Granville Historical Society Archives

The farm of the Goodrich family on North Street is now the site of the Denison University Homestead. The white house in 2004 stands on the northwest corner of North and New Burg. The bare fields in the left background are the site of today's Middle and High Schools.

The William T. Richards Family, courtesy of Patricia Battiston

The farm of A. A. Bancroft is best remembered for the abolitionist meeting of 1836. The farm as pictured here was owned by the Dustin family. The house stands at the North Street entrance to Denison University.

Granville Historical Society Archives

In and around the Village on smaller plats of land, families commonly raised vegetables, fruits, and poultry for home use. These hens provided eggs and meat for the Watkin family on Newark-Granville Road in the 1920s.

Granville Historical Society Archives

As many berries go in the mouth as in the bucket! In the Richards berry patch in 1934.

The William T. Richards Family, courtesy of Patricia Battiston

Mrs. Sidney Hollingworth in the garden at 337 West Broadway in 1942. She is standing in the midst of lima bean "teepees" with wax bush beans in front.

Sidney Hollingworth, courtesy of Florence Hollingworth Wright

Samples of Mrs. Hollingworth's domestic art. Some of the preserved produce included cherries, pickled onions, blackberries, beets, beans, tomatoes and mincemeat.

Sidney Hollingworth, courtesy of Florence Hollingworth Wright

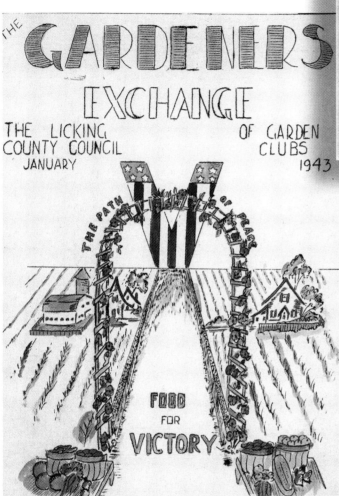

29. Victory Garden of 135 x 60 *McStanley family loan Home*

In addition to feeding a family of ten with fresh vegtables including: lettuce, spinach, radishes, peas, beans, beets, carrots, Swiss chard, cabbage, corn, parsley, potatoes, tomatoes, watermelons, muskmelons, and celery. We have canned 60 quarts tomatoes, 3 gals chili sauce, and frosted (after processing) 60 quarts green peas and 60 qts. string beans

Sample of an entry in the Granville Victory Garden Contest. Notice the amount produced in town on about one-fifth of an acre.

Granville Life-Style Museum

The Hollingworth garden on West Broadway in July, 1943.

(Above and left)
Sidney Hollingworth, courtesy of
Florence Hollingworth Wright

In 1943 when World War II was raging, the United States government urged all citizens to grow their own produce so that commercially prepared food could be used by allied troops. The result was the "Victory Garden" movement. Local garden clubs sponsored contests and published helpful guides to growing and preserving.

Granville Life-Style Museum

Florence Hollingworth and her father put up 52 quarts of wax beans and 21 glasses of berry jam while her mother was on vacation in the summer of 1943.

A young woman tends her flower bed, about 1890.

(Both images:)
Granville Historical Society Archives

Many homes were decorated outside with planters, climbing roses and vines, and blooming shrubs. This gentleman enjoys his "outdoor room' on North Plum Street in about 1915.

A member of the Watkin family in the garden at 1632 Newark-Granville Road in the 1940s.

Granville Historical Society Archives

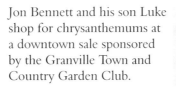

Jon Bennett and his son Luke shop for chrysanthemums at a downtown sale sponsored by the Granville Town and Country Garden Club.

The Granville Sentinel

The DeBow Brothers, Isaac and John, ran a marble works from 1859 to the 1930s. In this ca. 1864 view, the shop was located at the rear of the Methodist Church.

CHAPTER 4

Enterprise

The story of a town is the story of its enterprises. Even a farming community begins to need mills to grind grain and saw wood, brickyards and stoneyards to supply building materials, and stores to sell those things that no one can produce locally. As the population grows and becomes more town-centered, service-based industries expand apace. Restaurants, saloons, barber shops, and livery stables begin to fill needs undreamt of and unneeded by the first farming inhabitants. Next, new technologies give rise to new needs that produce new types of businesses. Telephone companies, telegraph offices, gas stations, and car repair shops are fitted into the fabric of the town. And from the first, bankers, lawyers, doctors, dentists, and teachers have been the professionals necessary for the good life of the inhabitants. Granville has a rich record of its enterprises, services, and professions.

Although the first inhabitants of Granville Township left no written records, the evidence of their enterprise remains. Their mounds and forts have amazed and perplexed residents almost from the beginning of white settlement. Stone tools and pottery shards still are turned up in backyards and fields. In the mid 1980s, a group of archaeologists, often aided by school students, excavated sites on the Munson Farm, now part of Erinwood on the north side of Newark-Granville Road. They found evidence of habitation dating back about 10,000 years. More recent Native American settlers made flint implements in the area.

Museum of the Granville Historical Society

"Within half a dozen years of its founding, Granville had become a manufacturing town. No fewer that eleven water-powered mills were built in the town's first quarter century—mills for lumber, for woolen manufacture, for grinding corn, and for making wheat flour. The Granville Furnace began forging iron pots and pans and plowshares as early as 1816. A cloth factory debuted in 1823. Distilleries and cider presses abounded: the town produced more whiskey at one point than the market could bear. Tanneries, brickyards, hatmakers, shoemakers, furniture-makers, stone quarrymen and cutters, and even a clockmaker could be found in early Granville. The first bank had made its appearance by 1815 and a full-fledged general store by 1817, as well as a popular inn. Altogether, early Granville was a pretty noisy, smelly, busy and ambitious place—a town for sure!"

—Dale Knobel in "The Importance of Village Life in Early Ninteenth-Century Ohio," *The Historical Times,* vol. XVI #2

(Both images)
Granville Historical Society Archives

This map by Estella Clouse White shows the group of businesses that once clustered on the canal feeder at the south end of Clouse Lane. Most of the channel and shops were obliterated by the construction of Route 16. The railway is now the bike path from Newark to Granville. Arbutus Ridge is now overlooked by the Park Trails development. *Map not to scale.*

"Wednesday, June 11 (1834) In the morning walked to the iron foundry one half a mile from the village thro pleasant fields, and a short piece of woods. We climbed one fence by the way. The ore is heated 120 days before it reaches its height. The furnace is 9 feet in diameter at its base & one foot at the top. I think it is 36 feet high. The wall is immensely thick, but the heat of ten months renders it useless & the masons from all the country round engage in repairing it for another blast. After it becomes hot, 1000 bushels of charcoal are used in a day. They have a pair of bellows. One is moved by water, the other by steam. The molds are made of wet sand. Patterns of iron or wood are put into the sand & drawn out again. Liquid fire is then poured in from ladles. In a few minutes the framing is removed and the articles are taken out and brushed. The men who lade out the iron have the sleeve of the right arm wet. Dutch ovens and teakettles are manufactured here. $40,000 worth in a year."

—Diary of Elizabeth Hubbard

Denison University Archives

A drawing of the Granville Furnace as it may have appeared in 1830. Drawing by an Everett family member.

Courtesy of Mary Ellen Everett

A stove and an urn manufactured at the Granville Furnace. The urn once graced the fine garden of Mrs. Anthony Prichard. Mrs. Prichard gave the urn to Hiram LaFerre, who as a child had greatly admired the garden.

Museum of the Granville Historical Society

Tannery Hill, now 635 Newark Road, built 1806-1810. Two Granville authors who lived in the tannery house when young—Ellen Hayes and Minnie Hite Moody— wrote lovingly about playing in the nearby fields and creek. Ellen Hayes' father was the tanner in the employ of Spencer and Edwin Wright in the 1850s and 60s. At that time the tannery proper was a two-storied, many-windowed building where hides were spread out to dry. The tannery shed covered four great acid-filled holes in the ground where the tanning process took place. These buildings were immediately to the west of the house. Minnie Hite Moody's grandfather purchased the property in the 1870s when the tanning business had ceased, and he filled in the vat holes for the safety of his family.

Granville Historical Society Archives

TO OUR PATRONS.

—

THE first volume of THE WAN-
DERER is nearly expired, and many of our subscribers, notwithstanding
the reasonableness of our terms, are
yet in arrears. We will still receive, as
full payment for the first volume,

Three Bushels of Wheat,
Eight Bushels of Corn,
Ten Bushels of Oats,
Twenty lbs. Butter,
Twenty lbs. Sugar,
Twenty-four lbs. Honey,
Two cords green Wood,
Five hundred lbs. good Hay,
Four lbs. good Wool,
67 lbs. good Beef, or Pork,
Six lbs. Bees Wax,
Twenty-four lbs. Hog's Lard,
Two gallons Linseed Oil,
32 doz. Hen's Eggs,
Twenty lbs. good Bar Iron,
8 gallons Whiskey,
5 yds. good Tow Cloth,
50 good Oak or Chesnut Rails,
24 lbs. good Cheese,
16 lbs. good Flax,
Two dollars worth of Castings,
Four days chopping Wood, or
One Dollar and Fifty Cents in Cash.
☞ All who are delinquent on the
11th of March, will have Fifty Cents
added to the price of their papers, a-
greeably to the terms of subscription.
Granville, Feb. 20, 1823.   8sO

In the earliest days of Granville, cash to be paid for
goods and services was in very short supply. An
elaborate system of barter was in existence in which
raw materials or country produce could be traded
for other necessities. This advertisement from
The Wanderer, Granville's first newspaper, shows
the range of goods available and desired. Sereno
Wright, whose home was at the present 121 South
Main Street, was the publisher of *The Wanderer*.

NEW GOODS,

AND GREAT BARGAINS AT THE
Granville Cash Store!!

R PARSONS is now receiving direct
from the city of New York his Fall
and Winter supply of NEW GOODS,
comprising a very extensive assortment,
and being laid in at very reduced prices,
he is determined to give his customers
the full benefit of the advantage. He is
opening

BROAD CLOTHS

of various colors at reduced prices; also
Petershams, full'd Cloths, Sattinetts, &c.
&c. for men's and boys's fall and winter
CLOTHING.
Blue and brown Camblets and Plaids,
for Cloaks.
   He is also opening a great variety of
Ladies' Goods, comprising real French
imitation and English Merino Cloths;
Merino Circassians, from 25 cents up-
wards; Merino and Shibit shawls and
handkfs.; a large assortment of those
stout dark calicoes, from 7 cts. upwards.
   A superior assortment of Silks con-
sisting of stout yard wide, for 56 cents;
Goods ... at 37 cents; English and
Italian lutestring and French silks of su-
perior quality; LEGHORN, TUSCAN, and
STRAW BONNETS at bargains. Also, he
is receiving a large assortment of

Groceries,

among which are Coffee, superior young
Hyson Teas, from 50 to 69 cents per lb.,
Loaf and brown sugar; Pepper; Spice;
Ginger, Indigo, &c. &c.
   Also, Hardware, Queensware, Steel
Nails, and best Spanish *Sole Leather* at
20 cents per pound.
   ☞ Now, all who be-
lieve in the old saying,
that a penny saved is as
good as one earned, will do well to call
and examine the above assortment which
will always be shown with pleasure. No
deviation will be made from the prices
asked, and the principle of ready pay will
be strictly adhered to. Farmers' produce will always be received at the high-
est market prices.   Sept. 23, 1834.

An advertisement for Ralph Parsons' "cash
store" from the *Newark Gazette* for 1834.
Parsons opened his store in the front
room of his home at the southeast corner
of Mulberry and Broadway (number 1 on
the map below). At about this time the
Ohio Canal was beginning to connect
Granville to the rest of the country. Canal
workers provided a market for goods,
trade with the East and South became easier,
and cash was more readily available.

(Both images)

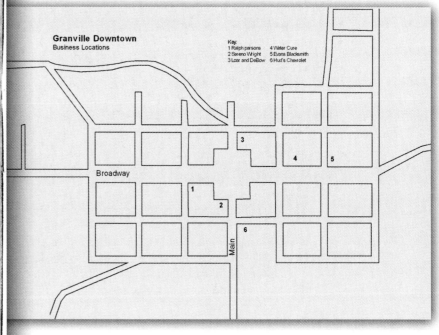

Granville Downtown
Business Locations

Key:
1 Ralph parsons   4 Water Cure
2 Sereno Wright   5 Evans Blacksmith
3 Loar and DeBow   6 Hux's Chevrolet

Broadway

Main

The gun shop of Benjamin Loar, before 1857. At the time this rare Daguerreotype was taken, the Loar shop was located to the north of the present Methodist Church. Note the crude wooden bridge in the left foreground crossing the ditch. Loar, who later had a shop on East Broadway, also sold and repaired watches, clocks, and jewelry.

Granville Historical Society Archives

A half stock percussion rifle with double set triggers made by Benjamin Loar in the 1870s.

Museum of the Granville Historical Society

Women were not often business proprietors until the twentieth century, unless they were milliners or dressmakers. Lorinda Munson Bryant (1855–1933) was an exception. She was widowed in 1886 when Charles Webster Bryant died at age 37. She took over the running of his drug store, studying chemistry and physiology at Denison University, then passing the state examination for registered pharmacist. Her abilities must have been impressive, for by 1890 she was chosen head of the science department at Ogontz College in Pennsylvania. After moving to New York City she published her first book in 1906, *Pictures and Their Painters—A History of Painting*, which was followed by several others on the subject of art.

(Both images)
Granville Historical Society Archives

Dr. William W. Bancroft established the Granville Water Cure in three buildings which he built next to his residence on East Broadway in 1852. He piped in spring water from Prospect Hill to use in his system of bathing and exercise for the treatment of chronic problems. The middle and right buildings shown are now 224 and 230 East Broadway. The house on the left was Bancroft's home at 222 East Broadway, since replaced by a bank building.

Granville Life-Style Museum

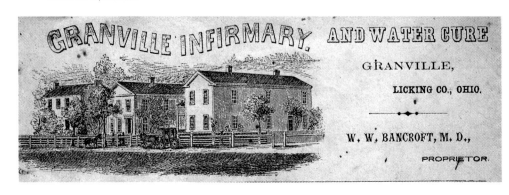

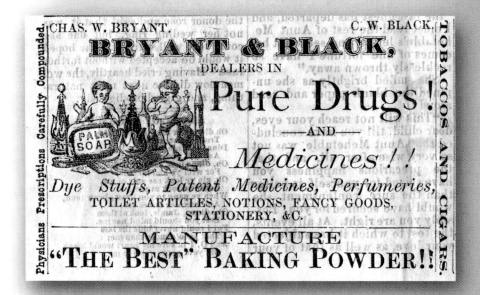

This pre-1880 photograph of the northwest corner of Broadway and Prospect seems to show the sealing of a business deal between the two gentlemen shaking hands. Note the shop of B.B. Loar on the extreme left. That small building, now 134 East Broadway, was replaced in the 1880s. The half-building marked "Prichard Brothers" was purchased by druggists Charles W. Bryant and Crayton W. Black in 1874. The drug store served as the village telegraph office and also as the home of the first telephone. Residents were sent for when a phone call came in for them.

Granville Historical Society Archives

Up and down the Broadway business block—circa 1900.

A view of the south side of the street from about 1910. St. Luke's and the Historical Society building are the only two that remain the same in 2004. The first building on the left was the brick home of Dr. A. K. Follett. Next was a small store that was at times a millinery shop and a barber shop. Third, with the long roofline, was the building housing Stuart's jewelry shop, Jones' meat market, and Futerer's bakery. Last before the Historical Society was a store used as a bakery, restaurant, and even a pool hall.

The man in the white apron stands in the present Historical Society building doorway. The tall building on the left was replaced by what in 2004 is the Park National Bank building at 119 East Broadway.

(All three images)
Granville Historical Society Archives

The interior of George Stuart's jewelry store. George Stuart and Gladys Jones are behind the counter.

Members of the George Futerer family and some passers-by on a rainy day. According to Minnie Hite Moody, the bakery sold cookies "for a penny apiece, the like of which have never been seen elsewhere, and may never again be seen this side of heaven." (*The Granville Sentinel,* April 14, 1983.) The Futerer bakery and the Stuart jewelry shop were located in the same long wooden building, which was destroyed by fire in 1927.

The Futerer/Rodes Family

Wetzel's Candy Kitchen at 122 East Broadway, now a newer building.

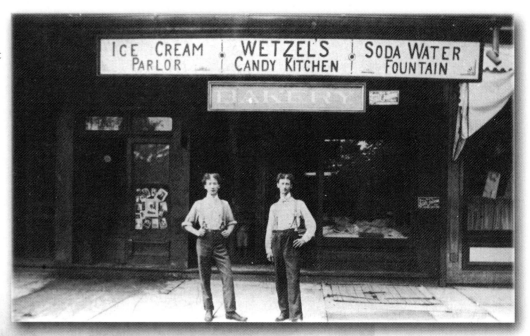

Mr. Wood stands outside his variety store at 124 East Broadway in about 1925.

The north side of Broadway. The building on the far left now has a third storey, added in the early 1900s. The next building was replaced by one of similar size. The rest of the block remains about the same in 2004.

(All three images)
Granville Historical Society Archives

Case's Candy Kitchen replaced Wetzel's business at the same address, but later moved to 130 East Broadway.

(Left and below)
Granville Historical Society Archives

Wright and Wright Grocery, 128 East Broadway.

Sam Morrow, Ann Vance, Cora Evans, and Roe Morrow stand outside Morrow and Son drygoods store at 132 East Broadway.

Granville Life-Style Museum

Advertisements from *The Granville Graphic* of 1874.

(All images on this page and facing page)
Granville Historical Society Archives

Byron Evans' blacksmith shop in the first block of North Pearl, east side. There were no fewer than ten blacksmith shops and livery stables in Granville's past. At least one of the blacksmiths made the natural transition to automobile repairing beginning about 1912.

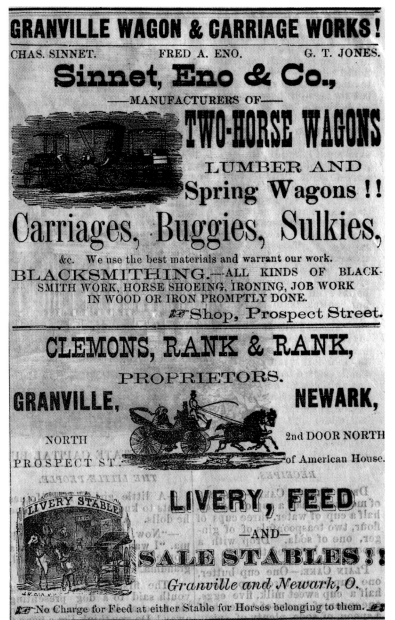

PROTEST

TO THE OHIO OIL COMPANY:-

On Tuesday evening, July 19th, 1 9 3 2, your District Manager, Mr. Ray W. Palmer, after the second of a series of THREE SPECIAL MEETINGS at which many citizens of GRANVILLE, OHIO, expressed their disapproval of the invasion of GRANVILLE, OHIO, by gas filling stations, made this statement to members of the GRANVILLE, OHIO, council : " If the people of GRANVILLE, or the council of GRANVILLE, don't want us to come in with a filling station, we'll stay out. "

Now, therefore, we, adult citizens of GRANVILLE, OHIO, do respect-fully protest to THE OHIO OIL COMPANY that we are inflexibly opposed to the invasion of our village by additional gasoline filling stations.

Granville has been home to numerous filling stations. This was perhaps the smallest. It stood diagonally at the southwest corner of Broadway and Cherry Street.

One page of a petition signed by many of the town's leading citizens in opposition to "the invasion of our village by additional gasoline filling stations," 1932.

"Hud" Williams owned a Chevrolet dealership at 113 East Elm in the 1940s and 1950s. During that era the unveiling of each year's new models was an occasion of great drama.

The Williams Family

This auto repair shop opened onto "Petunia Park," the open space in the rear of the businesses on the north side of Broadway, from the 1920s until the 1970s.

(Below and left)
Granville Historical Society Archives

Business in the second half of the 20th century.

Several small groceries, pharmacies and banks were the business focus during the second half of the 1900s. John Huffman, Carl Welsh, Tom Fuller, "Buck" Sargent, and Phil and Gib Blackstone were prominent among the grocers. Harold Taylor, Jim Scott, Louis and Greg Ream, and Bob Young all owned pharmacies. With the added convenience of hardware stores, clothing and gift shops, and book and office supply stores, Granville was indeed a location for "one trip" shopping.

Oese Robinson, Harold Taylor, and Elizabeth Taylor in Taylor's pharmacy. The Robinson family owned the buildings at 130, 132 and 134 East Broadway for over 100 years.

Granville Life-Style Museum

John Huffman poses for a 1940s advertisement.

Granville Historical Society Archives

Tom Fuller at his meat counter in the 1970s. Tom also featured cheese and imported baskets in his store at 128 East Broadway.

(Both images)
Granville Historical Society Archives

FULLER'S MARKET

CALL YOUR ORDER . . . . PHONE 8212

EVERY DAY DELIVERY SERVICE

CRANBERRY SAUCE, 1 lb. cans, 2 for 35c

Two Jars For The Price of One.
BORDEN'S INSTANT COFFEE _____ 49c

Chase and Sanborn Instant
COFFEE, 1 jar, 45c—2 jars _____ 50c

Our Contest Continues With $10.00 Free Merchandise
Better Try Your Skill

We Redeem All Your Soap Coupons

SARGENT'S MEAT MARKET

HOME DRESSED MEATS

MEET US FOR GOOD MEAT

PHONE DIAL 8215

Time to Fill Your Locker and Home Freezer!

Before You Fill Your Locker or Home Freezer

Contact Us For Beef, Pork, Veal, and Lamb by the

Quarter, Side or Carcus.

We Also Do Processing

For Lockers and Home Freezers.

Photo: *The Granville Sentinel*

Buck and Dora Sargent were followed by the Blackstone family in the meat business at 126 East Broadway.

(All three images)
Granville Historical Society Archives

Carl Welsh and his grocery store at 116 East Broadway.

(All three images)
Jennifer Welsh

Welsh's Grocery

Special For Friday and Saturday

GOLD MEDAL
FLOUR _____5 lb. bag 43c

No. 1 MAINE
POTATOES _____ 50 lb. bag $1.89

KETCHUP, Lg. bottle, _____2 for 29c

CHASE AND SANBORN
INSTANT COFFEE, 45c jar, _____2 for 45c

ORDER YOUR THANKSGIVING POULTRY FROM

WELCH'S GROCERY

PHONE 8230   WE DELIVER

Martha and Carl Welsh inside the store with Pat, Jim, and Nancy in 1949.

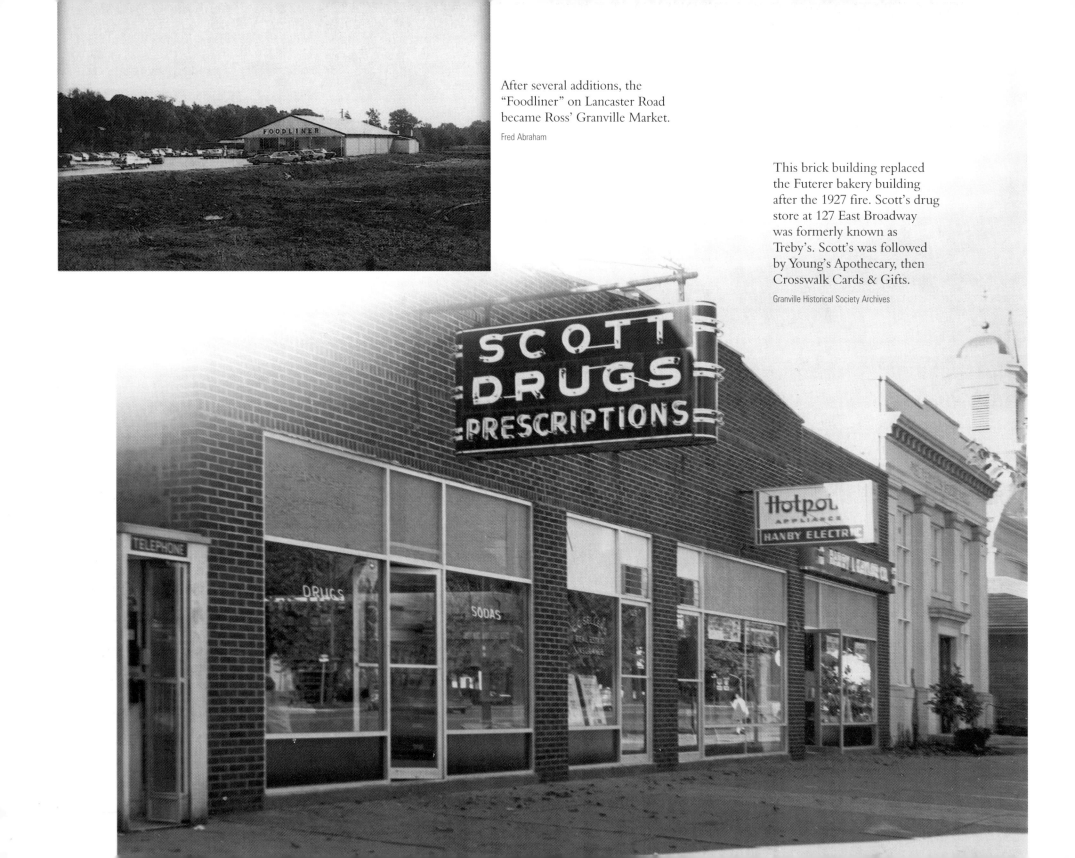

After several additions, the "Foodliner" on Lancaster Road became Ross' Granville Market.

Fred Abraham

This brick building replaced the Futerer bakery building after the 1927 fire. Scott's drug store at 127 East Broadway was formerly known as Treby's. Scott's was followed by Young's Apothecary, then Crosswalk Cards & Gifts.

Granville Historical Society Archives

The familiar north side of Broadway in the mid-1950s.

Granville Historical Society Archives

The same view about 45 years later.

Granville Village Planning Department

This imposing set of buildings stood at the northeast corner of Broadway and Prospect until 1967. Gregory's Hardware fills the shops at street level in this ca. 1960 photo. Gregory's Toyland was a favorite stop for the children of Granville, especially as Christmas drew near. "The toy store was heaven on earth for us kids and often a dismay to grownups. Our favorite purchases were squirt guns and pea shooters." Steve Smith in *The Granville Sentinel*, March 24, 1983.

(Both images)
Granville Historical Society Archives

SELECT

YOUR XMAS

TOYS NOW

● Electric Trains
● Mechanical
   Trains
● Bicycles
● Tricycles
● Metal Doll
   Houses
● "Baby Coo"
   Dolls
      Cries, Sobs and Coos
● Wetting-
   Drinking Dolls
● Stuffed Animals
● Wagons
      All Sizes
● Desks
● All Kinds
   of Games

GREGORY'S

TOYLAND

The set of buildings at Broadway and Prospect came down in 1967.

Granville Historical Society Archives

Fill 'er up? The hotel and hardware buildings were followed by Don Bennett's Colonial Marathon service station.

The Granville Sentinel

By 2001, Broadway and Prospect had changed again. Greg Ream moved his Taylor's drug store to a new building on the corner. (See pages 182 and 183.)

Granville Village Planning Department

An Everett School has stood on or near this site on Alexandria road since Agnes, Israel, and Elizabeth Everett deeded a plot for a school in 1836. This brick schoolhouse was built in 1883 and is now a private residence.

Granville Historical Society Archives

CHAPTER 5

Education and the Business of Education

THE FIRST SCHOOL HOUSE. 1805.

Three weeks after the main party of immigrants arrived in Granville in November 1805, a committee was appointed to establish a school for the eighty children. They built a large, sturdy log cabin, which also served as a meeting house. By 1809, a frame school house with glass windows had taken its place, and in 1820 a three-storey brick school was erected at the north end of Main Street. The adjacent sketches of the first log school house, the 1809 frame building, and the 1820 brick school were drawn from the memories of early settlers. The log building was furnished with slab benches and tables fastened to the walls and used for all community meetings and worship services. The 1809 structure, on the site of the present Methodist Church, had glass windows and was plastered and heated. It also served as the meeting house for the Congregational Church. Tradition says that the school children faced their teacher at one end of the building and the congregation faced the other end for Sunday services. The swampy site that had been a pond made the small bridge to the doorway necessary.

The 1820 brick building also accommodated the Masonic Hall on the top storey. By 1854 this building was outgrown and the Village acquired land on Granger Street for a new building.

In 1854 a commodious brick school was built on Granger Street. Olive Maxwell Dowell, who attended the school in the 1880s, sketched this floor plan from her memories of classes there.

(Both images)
Granville Historical Society Archives

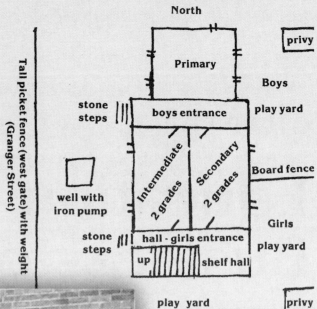

North

privy

Primary

Boys

play yard

stone steps

boys entrance

Intermediate 2 grades

Secondary 2 grades

Board fence

well with iron pump

Tall picket fence (west gate) with weight (Granger Street)

Girls play yard

stone steps

hall - girls entrance

up

shelf hall

play yard

privy

Children from the lower grades outside the old brick building, about 1880.

In 1888 classes for Granville children were held in the Town Hall and other buildings while the new Union School rose on the Granger Street site of the 1854 school. This view was taken about 1920.

Granville Historical Society Archives

The Granville High School Class of 1905 in the doorway of the Union School. Members of the Class were: Ada B. Hankinson, Hugh C. Tyler, Gertrude L. Williams, Ada E. Chrysler, Gertrude E. White, Elizabeth C. Futerer, Helen W. Keller, Elizabeth A. Barret, Josephine B. Williams, James Harry Forsythe, Anna C. Lewis, Faye Hulshizer, Ina Isabelle Bishop, Jeanette M. Futerer, Shirley Slack, Lena B. Griffin, Lenna Mae Bishop, Nora Belle Richards, Parry R. Jones, Ethal L. McMillen, and Alice M. Avery.

High School commencements were held in the Opera House.

(All three images)

Granville Historical Society Archives

The Granville High School band, about 1916. Dick Howe is at the right in the front row. Minnie Hite holds her trombone, sixth from the right in the back row. Dick Howe was a Professor of Physics at Denison and a champion of Granville's history. Minnie Hite Moody became a well known author and writer for *The Atlanta Journal and Constitution.* Granville residents cherished her "I Remember, I Remember" columns written after she retired to Granville.

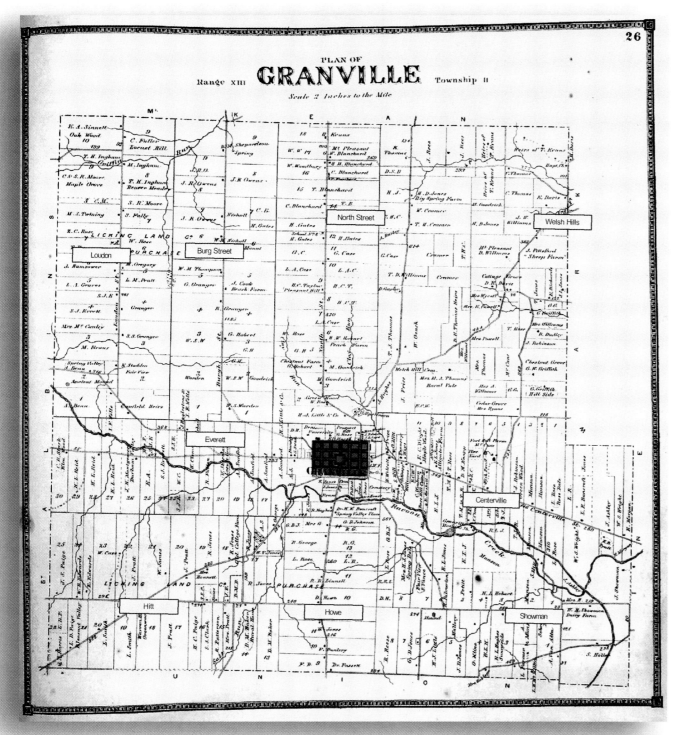

Until the nine rural school districts were consolidated with the Granville town schools in 1920, students living outside town usually attended their local district schools. Ellen Hayes remembers commencing her formal education in the old stone octagon shaped school on Centerville Street. No image of this school survives to augment her description:

"One side of the octagon contained the front door, opposite which was the teacher's desk, with a small blackboard for background. On the other six sides were desks, high and wide and immovable, with long wooden benches. Seats for the younger scholars were provided just in front of the big desks. These seats were narrow, unpartitioned, and built as part of the desks. Thus the little folks had to sit there without desks of their own, without arm-supports or the least provision for storing away their few belongings. . . A queer upright stove occupied the centre of the room and bituminous coal was burnt."

This frame Centerville School replaced the Octagon School. This faded photograph is the only image that survives. Carrie Little remembered her first teacher, Sarah Foote, fondly, despite her novel punishments. "When twelve or more failed in their recitations, the boys were told to put on the girls sun bonnets, and the girls the boys hats, and march through the street to Mr. Linnels."

(All four images)
Granville Historical Society Archives

Lulu Howard, in the doorway, and her pupils in the Hitt School on the Columbus Road, about 1914.

Thomas Blanchard purchased the lot for the North Street School in 1867. The brick building replaced the original frame structure in 1891. After 1924, it was long used for storage by the Breymaier family, and is now a private home.

The 1866 *Atlas of Licking County* shows a school on this site. The present building was apparently built in 1871. Alpha Palmer purchased the Howe School in 1924 for $500. It has been renovated as a private residence.

In 1899, the brick Welsh Hills School building replaced a frame school built in 1858. The 1825 capstone from the Old Stone School was set into the gable end. It became the school for Granville Sub-district 9. The Welsh Hills Grange purchased the building in 1924 after the Granville Township Schools were consolidated. Later it was used as a private residence and was demolished in 1981.

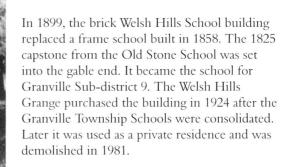

Students living in the Welsh Hills rode this bus to the consolidated school in Granville in 1928.

Jennifer Welsh

The ruins of the Old Stone School on Welsh Hills Road.

(Left and top)
Granville Historical Society Archives

Granville High School on Granger Street in 1924. This building, with additions and remodeling, served as the high school and then the middle school for some seventy years.

Granville Historical Society Archives

The 1924 section of the old school was demolished in 1997 after a new Granville High School was constructed on New Burg Street and middle school students moved into the earlier high school on New Burg. A section of the building was preserved and now houses the Board of Education for the Granville Exempted Village Schools. A private home is now on the former high school site.

The Granville Sentinel

The marching Blue Aces parade in Granville, September 1938.

(Left and bottom)
Granville Historical Society Archives

Members of the Granville High School Class of 1949 in December 1944. Pictured are: Front Row: Kenneth Johnson, Ndala Hall, Frances Kirkendal, Phyllis Carpenter, Florence Hollingworth. Second Row: Miss Miley, Patty Rolt-Wheeler, Marlene Borror, Emma Posey, Barbara Warrington, Anna Young, FredDowns. Back Row: Dick Spaulding, Earl Wilson, Dick Layton, Bob Moreland, Eugene Roberts, Walter Bricker, Tom Kier, John Brown.

Sidney Hollingworth, courtesy of Florence Hollingworth Wright

Students from Marian Mahard's fifth grade class ready to step off in the March of Dimes parade in 1952.

School's out. Erin Apacki and Gina Ormond, in front row, and Carrie Lloyd, Mary Kay Apacki, Courtney McCracken, and Lisa Trees, in second row leaving the elementary school in 1975.

Anestis Diakopoulos, used with permission

T-shirt day at Granville elementary school, 1983.

(All three images)
The Granville Sentinel

Blake Sheppard, Stephanie Ussery, and Ryan Harris using the new computers in the elementary school library while Carl Frazier, Executive Secretary of the Granville Foundation, watches. The school received a grant from the Granville Foundation to purchase computers for the elementary school in 1991.

Posing in the bus line.

Members of Granville's winning *In the Know* team in 1989. From left: Matt
Drake, Eric Evans, Ben Denton, Eric Freeman with their advisor, Bob Hill.

The Ace Moving and Singing Company, performing
at a Newark, Ohio, bank in 1989.

The Robert Drake Family

Emily Klauder, Abri Brickner and
Anna Schlichter as the Lollipop Guild
in the May 2001 Granville High School
production of the Wizard of Oz.

(Left and top)
The Granville Sentinel

Ben Dils running the 200 meter
for the Blue Aces, 1991.

(All three images)
The Granville Sentinel

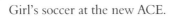

High School wrestling meet, 1997.

Girl's soccer at the new ACE.

Grading the Harmon-Burke playing field behind the Union School, now the site of the Granville Elementary School, on Granger Street. Opened in 1928, and financed by substantial gifts from E.G. Burke, the Harmon Foundation, and many donations from community members, the field served Granville for seven decades. In 1996, the Granville Boosters led a community effort to establish sports fields beside the new high school on New Burg Street. Harmon-Burke field now holds additional classrooms for the Granville Elementary School.

Courtesy of Mary Ellen Everett

Players raise their helmets in victory over Liberty Union, October 1996, the last game played on Harmon-Burke Field. The autographed ball used in that game is in the Granville Historical Society Museum.

The Granville Sentinel

The High School pep band marches up to The Ace, 1997.

A community-wide effort, "Moving Together" raised money and mobilized volunteers to provide new playing fields on New Burg Street beside the schools. At the dedication of the Blue Ace Field, known as "The Ace" a section of sod from Harmon-Burke Field was planted in the new field.

(Above and top right)
The Granville Sentinel

Granville High School in 2004.

William E. Holloway

The Jesse Munson house, built in 1810, on the way to a new life as the nucleus of the Welsh Hills School. (See page 29.)

(Above and bottom left)
The Granville Sentinel

Private schools occupy an important niche in Granville. The Welsh Hills School was founded in 1979 by Catherine Naul in the Welsh Hills northeast of Granville. By 1991, the school, then located in two houses in the Village, needed more space and launched a fundraising campaign to construct a new schoolhouse. The 1810 Jesse Munson house on Newark-Granville Road was available and threatened with demolition. It was purchased and moved a mile to the east to become the nucleus of the school in 1992. Dave Longaberger, CEO of the Longaberger Corporation, led the funding campaign and contributed labor and equipment to make the project a reality. Ground was broken to begin the renovation in 1994.

Middle school students at the Welsh Hills School engaged in cooperative research. The three divisions of the school each have their own space in the spacious schoolhouse. The children learn in small groups with an integrated curriculum.

(Left and bottom right)
Welsh Hills School

The Spring Hills Baptist church operates a Christian day school in their building on Newark-Granville Road. Pre-school children prepare for Thanksgiving in 1994.

Welsh Hills students enjoy the snow in front of the schoolhouse.

The early nineteenth-century settlers had hoped that Granville would become a mercantile or commercial center. They were on the main stagecoach road between Zanesville and Worthington. But the National Road was routed nine miles south of the Village in 1835, and the railroad passed four miles south in the 1850s. It became clear that the business of Granville would become education, and principally the education of other people's children. During the last two thirds of the nineteenth century, three institutions of higher learning flourished in Granville. The adjacent engravings from the 1875 *Atlas of Licking County, Ohio,* depict *(from top right clockwise)* the Granville Female College, The Young Ladies' Institute, and Denison University.

Granville Female College - Granville Ohio.
W. P. Kerr, A.M. Principal.

DENISON UNIVERSITY.
GRANVILLE LICKING CO.

(All three images)
Granville Historical Society Archives

Granville Female College

This building has served the community long and well. The Granville Congregational Church erected it in 1833 with a conference room in the basement and operated a Female Academy in the two upper floors. Enrollment in the Female Academy increased so rapidly that the school moved, in 1837, to a new building where the Granville Inn stands today. A Congregational Male Academy then held classes here. The Church had no further need for the building in 1863 and sold it to the Welsh Congregational Church who remodeled the building in Greek Revival style, converting its two stories into a single room with twelve foot windows. Welsh language services were held here for sixty years. Granville Grange No. 2230 purchased it for a grange hall in 1923, and sold it to the Granville Historical Society in 1973.

William P. and Harriet Bancroft Kerr in 1860.

By 1835 enrollment in the Congregational Female Academy had increased to the point that a larger building was needed. In 1837 the school moved to this four-storey building on Broadway where the Granville Inn now stands. The name of the institution was changed by state charter to the **Granville Female College** in 1867. William P. Kerr added the two-storey brick building to the left, at his own expense, in 1865. An able administrator and teacher, Kerr was the head of the college from 1854 to 1882. After his death the institution slowly declined and closed in 1898.

(All three images)
Granville Historical Society Archives

Teachers on the porch steps of the Granville Female College building, about 1890.

(All four images)
Granville Historical Society Archives

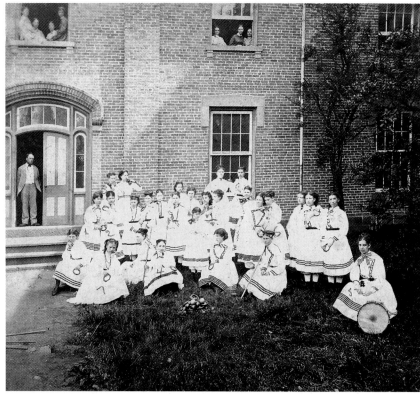

A group of students in their gymnasium dresses on the lawn in front of the Granville Female College, about 1870.

CONCERT

— BY THE —

Young Ladies of Granville Female College,

Tuesday Evening, June 18th, 1872.

PROGRAMME.

PART FIRST.

1. CHORUS—Song of Greeting,   ROOT.
2. OVERTURE TO TANCREDI—Eight Hands,   ROSSINI.
    Misses PUTNAM, A. KERR, CAYWOOD and ZOLLERS.
3. SONG—Marjorie's Almanac,   DOLBY.
    Miss ANNIE REBER.
4. PIANO SOLO—Polka Di Concert,   WALLACE.
    Miss LILLIE P. PUTNAM.
5. SONG AND CHORUS—The Beautiful Days that are Past, HOWARD.
    Miss KATE E. McDONOUGH.
6. PIANO DUETT—Restless Love,   KUNKEL.
    Misses ANNIE and EMMA REBER.
7. VOCAL SOLO—O waly, waly up the Bank,   BLUMENTHAL.
    Miss LOTTIE RICHARDS.

PART SECOND.

1. PIANO DUETT—Norma, (Two Pianos, Four Hands,)   ROSELLEN.
    Misses SAMPSELL and PUTNAM.
2. VOCAL SOLO—Leave me to Languish,   HANDEL.
    Miss KATE E. McDONOUGH.
3. SONG AND CHORUS—Softly fall the Silvery Moonbeams, PERSLEY.
    Miss LIZZIE F. CAYWOOD.
4. PIANO SOLO—Caprice Fantastique,   WOLLENHAUPT.
    Miss JOSEPHINE E. SAMPSELL.
5. VOCAL DUETT—Rhine Maidens,   GLOVER.
    Misses KERR and ZOLLARS.
6. BALLAD—Willie's Ship,   TOURS.
    Mrs. MARY ABBOTT THRESHER.
7. PIANO SOLO—Irish Diamonds,   PAPE.
    Miss ROSA L. KERR.
8. CHORUS—Happy and Light, from "Bohemian Girl," BALFE.

DOORS OPEN AT 7 O'CLOCK. - CONCERT COMMENCES AT 8 O'CLOCK.

ADMISSION. - - 25 CENTS.

Concerts or other programs given by college girls were public events, well attended by Granville citizens. The students were very well chaperoned. A common sight in town was the students from either the Female College or the Young Ladies' Institute marching two by two, with teachers at the front and rear of the file, on their way to church or to an event in the Opera House.

Granville Female College

REV. D. B. HERVEY, *President.*

Granville, Licking County, Ohio

A School for Young Ladies

LITERATURE,
    CLASSICS,
       ART, MUSIC

SPECIAL ADVANTAGES.

Latin, French and German without extra charge.
A Four Years' course in English Literature.

PREPARES FOR WELLESLEY.

STEAM HEATING.

EXPENSES MODERATE.

For further information address the President.

Return in Ten Days to
Box 1040 - - GRANVILLE, OHIO.

An envelope, used in the 1890s, promoting the advantages of the college.

This large plaque in the Granville Public Library commemorates the Granville Female College.

GRANVILLE FEMALE COLLEGE
MEN DIE. IDEALS LIVE.
ON THIS SPOT IN 1827, ONE OF THE FIRST
INSTITUTIONS IN AMERICA FOR THE HIGHER
EDUCATION OF WOMEN WAS STARTED.
IN 1833 IT WAS ORGANIZED AS
GRANVILLE FEMALE ACADEMY
IN ITS OWN BUILDING ON THE SOUTHWEST
CORNER OF ELM AND MAIN STREETS. IN
1836 IT WAS MOVED TO A FOUR STORY
BUILDING ON EAST BROADWAY.
IN 1861 IT'S NAME WAS CHANGED TO
GRANVILLE FEMALE COLLEGE.
IT MAINTAINED AN UNINTERRUPTED
AND HONORABLE HISTORY UNTIL 1898,
WHEN IT CLOSED IT'S DOORS.
1827
PRINCIPALS
REV. JACOB LITTLE, D.D.
MISS ELIZABETH GRANT   MISS MARGARET E. THEAKER
MISS NANCY BRIDGES   WILLIAM P. KERR, A.M.
MISS HANNAH BAILEY   MRS. SUSAN M. KERR
WILLIAM D. MOORE, A.M.   REV. DWIGHT B. HERVEY, PH.D.
WILLIAM P. KERR, A.M.   REV. EDWIN W. CHILDS.
REV. GEORGE H. WEBSTER   MISS CLARA SHELDON
1898

The influence of the Granville Female College lived on in its alumnae, not only in Granville but as they moved to distant parts of the world. Ten of the twelve members of the Class of 1874 returned for their reunion in 1905. Many of these women distinguished themselves in their life's work. In this photograph each holds her student picture. In the back row, from the left are: Lorinda Munson Bryant, Abby Kerr Colwell, Emma White Campbell, Dora Loar Henderson, Evalina S. Robinson, Helen Stark Munro, and Amanda Wilkin Huston. Seated in front are: Evaline Hurd Metcalf, Thalia Amelia Tight Ralston, and Sarah Follett Jones. Photos of the two absent members, Mary Smithyman McClane and Maude Edgerton Garvin are held on the laps of Lorinda Bryant and Amelia Ralston.

The Young Ladies' Institute—Shepardson College

Education for women under Baptist auspices in Ohio owes much to Charles Sawyer, a saddler by trade, who arrived in Granville in 1817. He was a generous donor and supporter in the establishment of the Granville Literary and Theological Institution, which became Denison University (see page 94). Within a year of the opening of that men's school, Sawyer purchased seven lots on the present corner of West Broadway and Plum Streets to establish a women's college. With his own funds he erected a building and hired Mrs. Jerusha Gear to teach until the arrival of Mr. and Mrs. James Poland from Massachusetts. Classes in the Granville Female Seminary began in December 1832.

An advertisement in both the *Newark Advocate* and the *Baptist Weekly Journal* for March 1, 1833, advised that instruction would be given in Orthography, Reading, Penmanship, Arithmetic, English Grammar, and Modern Geography for $3 a quarter. $4 a quarter would be charged for History, Ancient Geography, Natural History, Rhetoric, Composition, Logic, Algebra, Geometry, Chemistry, Astronomy, Latin, Greek, and Moral and Intellectual Philosophy. Board with private families was $1.25 a week.

In 1834 Charles Sawyer built a three-storey frame building on the north side of the block for a dormitory. His effort to raise an endowment from the Baptist denomination failed, and, suffering financial reverses, he was forced to sell the school to the Episcopal denomination and leave Granville. The Episcopalians operated the Granville Female Seminary in the same location until 1861, when it was purchased by Marsena Stone. He transferred a revived Baptist school for women, started by Mrs. Sarah Burton in the Baptist Church, and renamed it **The Young Ladies' Institute**.

In this 1868 photograph, you see Charles Sawyer's original building at lower right. The 1834 dormitory is in the center, with a fourth storey added by Marsena Stone clearly visible. Stone Hall, on the corner of Broadway and Plum, replaced the two white houses in 1905. Burton Hall replaced the dormitory building in 1888. The original building burned in 1900.

(Both images)
Granville Historical Society Archives

Dr. Daniel Shepardson purchased the Young Ladies' Institute from Marsena Stone in 1868, and he and his wife, Eliza Smart Shepardson, completely refurbished the buildings. This photograph shows the Y.L.I. Class of 1869 with Dr. Shepardson in the doorway of the original classroom building.

Mary O. Brooks taught at the Young Ladies' Institute from 1868 to 1887. She inspired her pupil Amelia Dixon, who graduated in 1882, to become a teacher. "Millie" Dixon was an orphan from Illinois who felt at home in the Y. L. I. She wrote in 1943, "Of my teachers I think Miss Brooks left the deepest imprint. From her, I got a passable knowledge of Math; in her Botany instruction, a love of Nature Study. From her optional instruction in 'Geography of the Heavens' I got inspiration. It was a joy to go out with her on clear nights to scan the star-spangled heavens and have her point out the constellations. Miss Brooks is inscribed on Orion for me."

(Both images)
Denison University Archives

Relaxing in a dormitory room before bedtime.

In 1886, Dr. Shepardson retired and sold the Y. L. I. to the Baptist denomination. In his honor, they renamed the school **Shepardson College**. In an agreement with Denison University, the Denison President administered both institutions. Classes in each college were open to both men and women, but Shepardson students continued to live on their campus and to receive their own degrees. Shepardson students were assigned to a table with a faculty member for meals. These women ate at Miss Amy Lyon's table in 1890. She later married Charles Eddy and lived in Granville. From the left, First row: Corona Walker, Mable Swartz, Anna Stevens. Middle Row, Flossie Boynton, Laura Sutton, Amy Lyon. Standing: Birda De'Armond, Harriet Davis, Rena Raymond.

(All three images)
Denison University Archives

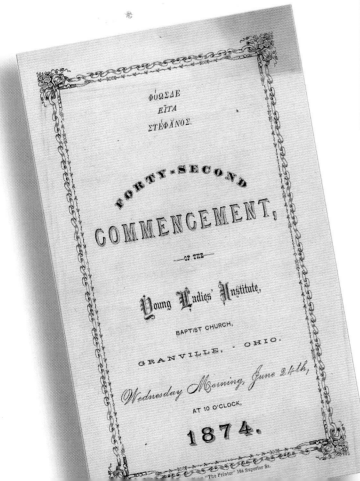

ΦΩΣΔΕ
ΕΪΤΑ
ΣΤΕΦΆΝΟΣ.

FORTY-SECOND

COMMENCEMENT,

—— OF THE ——

Young Ladies' Institute,

BAPTIST CHURCH,

GRANVILLE, - OHIO.

Wednesday Morning, June 24th,

AT 10 O'CLOCK,

1874.

Commencements were held at the Baptist Church. The Greek at the top of the cover page is translated "To the light, and then a crown." Greek and Latin were standard in the classical curriculum, so many people in the audience would have been able to read and understand this phrase.

A group of Shepardson girls outside Burton Hall in the late 1890s.

Courtesy of Duane Dawley

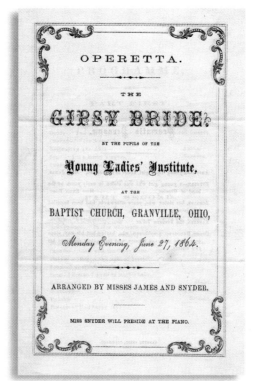

Students at the Young Ladies' Institute produced this operetta for the citizens of Granville in 1864.

Denison University Archives

In 1897, Professor Almon U. Thresher gave his spacious home on the corner of Broadway and Cherry Street to Shepardson College for use as a much needed Conservatory of Music. The gift, in memory of his wife, Mary Abbott Thresher, was on the site of the first Baptist Church built in Granville, in which the first classes of Denison University met in 1831. In 1898, the college added a Recital Hall onto the north end of Thresher Hall. Thresher Hall was taken down in 1959. Recital Hall remained until it was removed to make space for Burke Hall in 1972.

Granville Historical Society Archives

Denison University

Drawn by Henry Howe.

Henry Howe's 1846 drawing of Granville College, a mile south of Granville on the Columbus Road. It was established in 1831 as The Granville Literary and Theological Institution. In 1845 the name was changed to Granville College to reflect common usage. The college moved into Granville to the hill overlooking the village in 1854 and was chartered as **Denison University** in 1856 following a gift from William S. Denison of Muskingum County.

Henry Howe, *Historical Collections of Ohio*

A photograph of Denison University taken from Sugar Loaf in the late 1880s. The four buildings on the hill are from the left: a white frame, moved into town from the former college location on Columbus Road; a brick, later called Marsh Hall, erected on this site in 1856; a second brick building, later called Talbot Hall, erected in 1869; and Professor Marsh's home on the present site of Beth Eden. This house was moved to the south east corner of Mulberry and Elm before Beth Eden was built in 1901. The houses at the lower edge of the photo are on West Broadway. The corner of Broadway and Plum Street is at lower right.

Jonathan Going was the second President of the Granville Literary and Theological Institution but in many ways was responsible for its founding and its location in Granville. He came to Ohio in 1830 to work with the Baptist Education Society. He had been minister of a church in Worcester, Massachusetts, and a trustee of Amherst College. Described as warm hearted, friendly, and with a rare sense of humor, he could see that opportunities for education were nearly absent in the "West." He was concerned about training ministers but felt that a classical education was needed as a basis for theological instruction. In Granville he found men —such as Charles Sawyer (see page 90)—willing to work to found a school. It was envisioned as a "useful institution" to provide a classical education for young men. The Fairmont Theological Seminary in Cincinnati would provide Theological training.

Going continued his missionary work and was instrumental in founding Shurtleff, Franklin, and Kalamazoo colleges. In 1837 he returned to Granville at a time of financial crisis for the College. He had been offered the Presidency of Shurtleff College, but said that he knew of no one else willing to go to Granville and do the hard work necessary to ensure its success. Under his leadership and inspiration the college debt was nearly eliminated. He left a void when he died in office in 1844. The students raised funds to erect an large and handsome limestone monument for his grave in the Denison Cemetery.

(Left and above)
Denison University Archives

In 1878, a Denison library building was provided by William Howard Doane. The interior was one large room in the shape of a Greek cross. For the first time, all college library books were available in the same place. William H. Doane was a generous benefactor to Denison University. He and his daughters donated five buildings to Denison over the years, in addition to the Fannie Doane Home for missionary childen on West Broadway. His business in Cincinnati was machine tools, but his avocation was music. The tunes for many familiar gospel hymns came from his pen.

(Both images)
Denison University Archives

Zella Allen Dixson at work in the 1878 library. She had studied with Melvil Dewey at Columbia University and President Galusha Anderson brought her to Denison in 1887 to catalog the library using the Dewey system of classification. She was hired as the full-time librarian in 1888, and for the first time, the library was open all day. Book circulation jumped to 7000 in 1888.

A Denison Chemistry laboratory class during the 1898–99 school year. Dean Deeds is in the light jacket, second from the left. The man in the dark jacket and tie leaning against the desk is Wayland Marlow. He is looking across the aisle at Ruth Sharer in the dark dress and hat. They married two years later and became the parents of Mary Lou Marlow Koerner, who many Granvillians remember.

A fraternity card game, about 1900.

The girls of the Class of 1915 turn out to cheer their team.

The men of the Class of 1912 celebrate their victory at Scrap Day in 1908 by lining up on Broadway in the shape of their class year.

The Queen of the May is driven away in an automobile after her coronation in 1913.

Carnival Day at Denison in 1914 on the lower campus. The women of each class are dressed in distinctive garb.

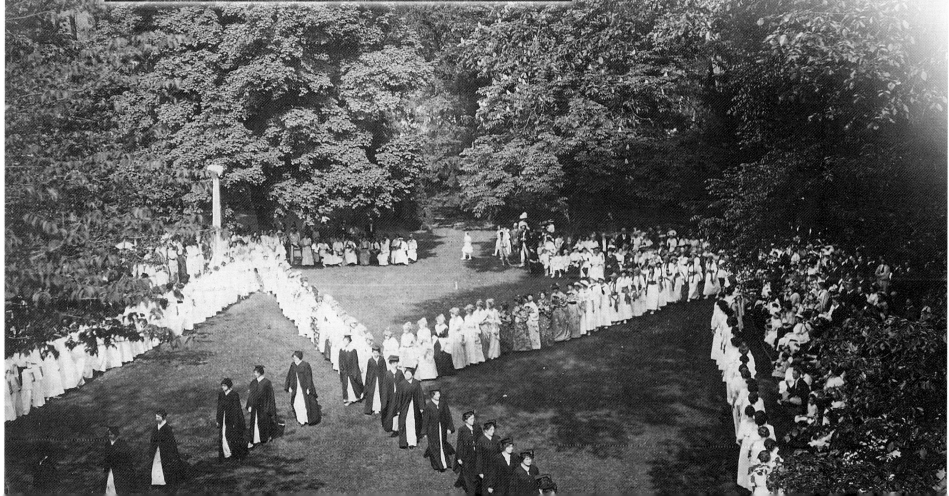

Grading the new road to Denison, 1868. Until then wheeled access to the campus had required climbing the Burg Street hill to a point near the present Shorney Hall. Professor Marsh, who lived on top of the hill, purchased several lots and laid out a curving road from Main Street to the College buildings on the hilltop. Fletcher O. Marsh gained a driveway to his home. Denison University gained a gracious entrance drive from the center of the village, known to generations of students as "The Drag."

Doane Academy building, which now houses Denison's administrative offices. The staircase and plaza were at the top of the entrance drive to the campus and led up to the academic quadrangle. This photograph was taken about 1920.

(All images on this page and facing page)
Denison University Archives

The 1891 Denison Baseball Team. It won all its games but one for two years. At that time, the team arranged its own schedule, bought its own equipment and uniforms, and found places to practice. One member of the team, Dan Daub the pitcher, went directly from Denison to the major leagues. He played for the Brooklyn Bridegrooms.

The studio of Denison radio station, WJD, in Barney Hall. Denison had one of the earliest commercial radio stations in the midwest. Denison Physics professor, Richard Howe, sponsored it to investigate the physical phenomenon of the projection of sound through space. The station also aired music with a player piano and broadcast Denison football games.

A "botanical outing" with breakfast on Arbutus Ridge.

A climbing tower was built in Spring Valley pool for the Naval Training unit training at Denison in 1944. They also enjoyed the pool and the local social scene.

Sailors in the V-12 training unit fill their trays under World War II posters in Shepardson Dining Hall, until that time exclusively for women. After Pearl Harbor most Denison men, both faculty and students, were drafted or enlisted in the armed services. To partially fill the void, service groups trained at Denison during the war years; first, a Pre-Meteorological Group, then V-12 and V-5 units of marines and sailors. The women students moved to Fraternity Row, the service units into the dormitories, and the annual calendar was completely re-arranged to military specifications.

(All images on this page and facing page)
Denison University Archives

The women's basketball team pose in their uniforms in 1917.

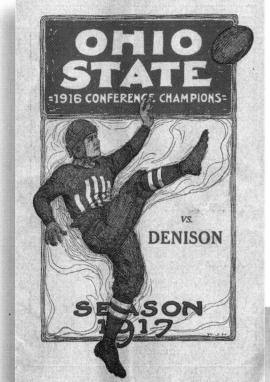

Denison vs Ohio State in 1917. Ohio State won this game handily but a dozen years earlier Denison had defeated them on two occasions. The two schools were of comparable size early in the 20th century.

Clearing the bar, 1923.

Denison cheerleaders practice on the campus in 1927.

A lacrosse game on the Denison campus in 1972. Lacrosse is one of the most popular sports at the college and the Denison women also field a team. In 2004 every student at Denison has access to sports and recreation. There are eleven varsity sports for men and eleven for women, in addition to "club" sports.

Wayne Woodrow Hayes played tackle on the Denison football team, was a member of the Sigma Chi fraternity, and graduated in the class of 1935 with a major in History. Woody served in the Navy during World War II and came back to coach at Denison in 1946. He led the team to a string of eighteen winning games beginning with the victory over Wooster in 1946. He moved to Ohio State in 1951 for a memorable career.

(All images on this page and facing page)
Denison University Archives

The Farewell to the Wigwam lunch, June 1949. The old Wigwam, built in 1924 to provide a standard basketball court, and used for many large gatherings, was demolished that summer. After World War II, Denison acquired two surplus airplane hangars and converted them to The Alumni Memorial Field House and Gymnasium on the north side of the College hill beside Deeds field.

Student life after the war was enlivened by veterans returning to the business of education and by the the construction of both dormitories and academic buildings. Here, students are leaving a required chapel service in the 1950s.

Students react to national and world events. A Viet Nam Day demonstration in November 1965.

A group of students in 1959 appealed to the "milk of human kindness" for charitable donations by parading a cow down Chapel Walk.

A class on the grass, a Denison tradition on beautiful days. Professor Don Valdes teaching a class on the campus in 1961.

(Both images)
Denison University Archives

The past three Presidents gathered for the inauguration of Dale T. Knobel, Denison's nineteenth President, in 1998. From the left: Dale T. Knobel, Michele Tolela Myers, Andrew G. De Rocco, and Joel P. Smith.

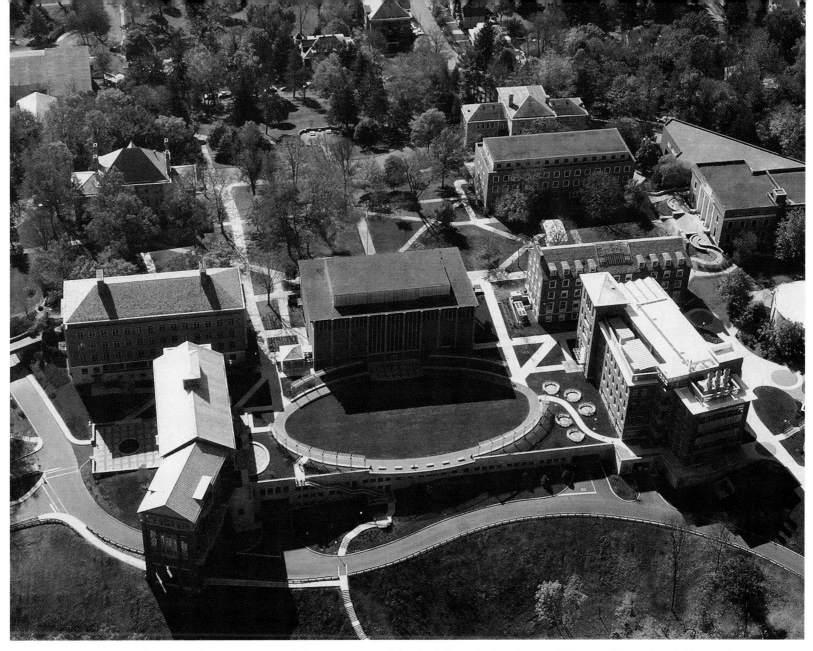

There have been many changes in the University and the appearance of the the hilltop during the past 150 years. The original 24 acres have increased to 1,200. In 1917 the size of the campus was increased five-fold by purchasing the rest of the hill and the athletic grounds to the north. Immediately, the Frederick Olmsted firm was asked to prepare a master plan which set the design for today's campus. In the 1960s land for a Biological Reserve, some 350 acres, was added to the north. Both classrooms and dormitory buildings have been erected and some buildings have been taken down. The present academic quadrangle has been essentially unchanged for the past fifty years, but major changes have taken place north of Slayter Student Union in the past five years. A new underground parking garage is topped by a green Common and flanked by two new buildings, the Burton D. Morgan Center on the east and the new Samson Talbot Hall of Biological Science to the west. This view looks south over the new Campus Common and the academic quadrangle toward the Village of Granville.

Denison University Resources and Public Affairs

"Our brave old Academic town,
    As all her children know!"

Churches dominate the Granville skyline on the cover of *"Granville, A Pleasant Memory"* published in 1899 by Thalia Amelia Ralston and William G. Tight.

(Facing page, top)
A scale drawing of the first frame Congregational Church building. The tall steeple was replaced with a lower rounded belfry in 1837.

(Facing page, bottom)
This drawing shows the 1831 brick Baptist Church which stood on the northeast corner of Broadway and Cherry Street. This church was still unfinished as opening exercises for the new Baptist college, which became Denison University, were held there in December 1831.

CHAPTER 6

Faith

The Granville settlers had faith in their God, faith in their country, faith in the future, faith that they would prosper after moving west into the wilderness, and faith in each other. They organized a new church of about thirty members, gathered like-minded neighbors into a company, and left their well established homes to journey to the "new lands" in Ohio. The first Sunday after their arrival in the Fall of 1805 they gathered around a felled beech tree to give thanks for safe passage. They found Welsh neighbors northeast of the village with their own meeting house. The first building in the new village served as school, church, and meeting place, but by 1816 the Congregational Church had put up a large frame building with an eighty-foot steeple. Other religious groups followed suit; a brick Baptist church in 1831, a Greek Revival Episcopal structure in 1837, and a new frame Baptist Church in 1849. In 1861, the Congregationalists built a brick church in the place where their old building had stood. In 1884, the Methodists built their new church on the northeast corner of the square. The steeple was topped by a slender spire, which was taken down by 1915. The churches and the schools founded by the churches shaped Granville in the nineteenth century and formed the community we see today.

The beautiful ceiling centerpiece in St. Luke's was rendered by Orren Bryant of St. Albans Township. On February 4, 1838, he wrote to his father in Massachusetts, "I have taken a job lathing and plastering an Episcopal meeting house in Granville which gives me employment this winter. I have a good stove and it will be a comfortable winter's job. The ceiling is to be paneled and ornamented with a centerpiece and enriched moulding in stucco. . . I have three hundred and twenty five dollars for doing the job. I have the winter before me. . . it is to be completed by the first day of June. . . I hope to make a good job of it."

The parishioners of St. Luke's Episcopal Church obtained the services of Benjamin Morgan to design their church in the Greek Revival style. The interior is enhanced by the original brass chandelier and beautiful plaster motifs. Both the chandelier and the belfry bell were shipped from Philadelphia. Morgan advised Orren Bryant in a letter of August 3, 1839, to raise the dome on the steeple three inches before starting the dome, so that it would appear to be a semicircle from the ground.

(Above and inset)
Granville Historical Society Archives

The ceiling medallion and chandelier in St. Luke's as the chandelier was being re-hung after it was refurbished in 2001.

The Granville Sentinel

The house that split the Church. The well-liked Congregational minister, the Reverend Ahab Jinks, began building this house in 1823. With winter approaching, he was concerned about completing the brick laying before freezing weather began. Describing it as a "work of necessity," he authorized the masons to work on Sunday. Many members of his congregation were appalled at this desecration of the Sabbath, and meeting after meeting followed with positions hotly defended. The division in the church finally led to the formation of a second Congregational church. A significant faction organized a Presbyterian Church. When Jinks was called to account, he refused to yield, and withdrew to join the group planning to establish an Episcopal Church. This group met with itinerant ministers for several years before building St. Luke's in 1837. The house at 124 South Main, with several additions, is now a real estate office.

Granville Historical Society Archives

The Reverend Jeremiah Hall, pastor of the Baptist Church, can claim much credit for keeping Denison University in Granville when it was threatened with "removal" to a more promising community. He formed a group to raise funds to purchase the Prichard property on the hill north of town and move the college there. The college elected him President and he is credited with soliciting a pledge of $10,000 from William S. Denison of Muskingum County. Granville College was renamed Denison University and remained in Granville, greatly influencing the future course of the community.

The 1849 Baptist Church as it stood on the southwest corner of the public square. The growth of both Baptist schools and parishioners in the community hopelessly crowded the 1831 building by mid-century. William Warden, a master builder, designed and built the new church in the Greek Revival style. By the 1880s it, too, was overcrowded. The congregation erected a new stone church on this site and moved the old building across Main Street. It became the town hall and was long known as the Opera House.

Granville Historical Society Archives

Denison University Archives

ON THIS SPOT
WAS ERECTED IN 1809
THE FIRST MEETING HOUSE OF
THE WELSH HILLS BAPTIST CHURCH.

HERE ALSO WAS ORGANIZED IN 1811
THE MUSKINGUM BAPTIST ASSOCIATION.

THE CHURCH WAS ORGANIZED SOME 40 RODS
EAST IN THE CABIN OF DAVID THOMAS, SEPT. 4
1808, WITH THE FOLLOWING MEMBERS, VIZ.

THEOPHILUS REES,   ELIZABETH REES,
DAVID THOMAS,   MARY THOMAS,
THOMAS POWELL,   ELIZABETH JAMES,
DAVID LOBDELL,   JOSHUA LOBDELL,
        NATHAN ALLYN.

PROPOSED BY T. J. THOMAS.
1886.

This stone tablet in the Welsh Hills Cemetery marks
the site of the first meeting house of the Welsh Hills
Baptist Church.

The Reverend Jacob Little, the conscience of the community,
served as pastor of the Congregational Church from 1827 to
1864. His energy and enthusiasm revived the splintered
church. Elizabeth Hubbard, who visited Granville in 1834,
described him. "He was a plain looking sensible man with
rather a vein for pleasantry. His wife, a very ordinary woman
in appearance & just as much at her ease as she could be.
Attended church in the afternoon, a plain looking building
filled with plain people who sat stiller & were vastly more
attentive than a city congregation with all their refinement.
Subject of the sermon—vain oblations—very practical &
plain & containing some interesting facts."

(All images on this page and facing page)
Granville Historical Society Archives

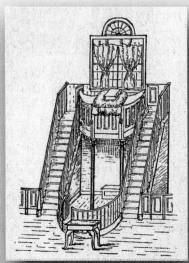

A drawing of the old
high pulpit in the 1816
Congregational Church.

The first Congregational Church (1816-1861), just before it was demolished to construct a
new church on the same site. Note the pile of lumber at the right of the picture. During the
period of construction, the congregation was welcomed into the other churches in town.

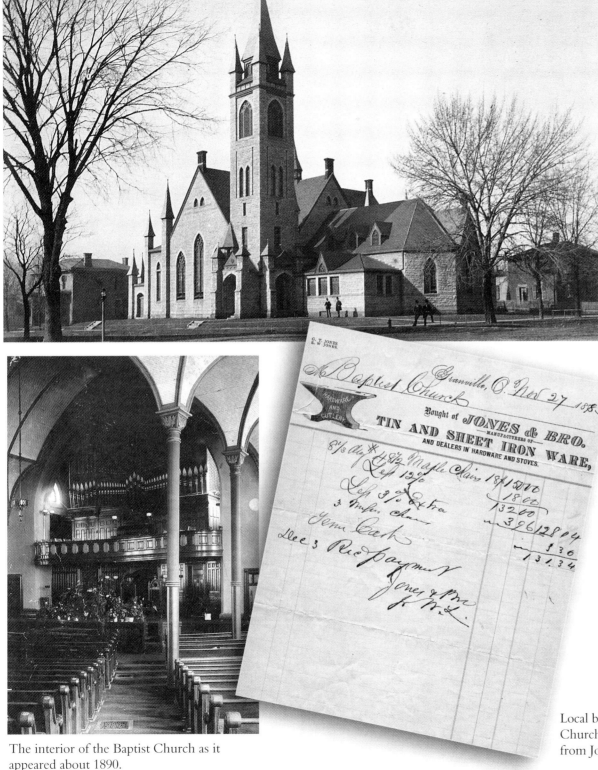

The new 1883 Baptist Church. Funds were raised in Baptist Churches throughout Ohio for "the student's church" to serve the students of Denison University and Shepardson College. It could accommodate 1000 persons. Students were expected and required to attend daily chapel services on campus and the church of their denomination on Sunday.

Dr. Charles J. Baldwin was a veteran of the Civil War, who still suffered from injuries. He served the Baptist Church from 1886 to 1913 and was noted as an inspiring preacher. His carefully handwritten sermons occupy twelve feet of shelving in the Granville Historical Society archives, each annotated with the date of delivery. William Utter says, "He was forced to give up a large city church in Rochester, New York, because his strength was not equal to the burden of such a ministry. In his later years he appeared to be quite frail as he sat, with a shawl draped over his shoulders, in his chair behind the pulpit, but when he arose to deliver his sermon he spoke as a man of great energy."

The interior of the Baptist Church as it appeared about 1890.

Local businesses were used to furnish the new Baptist Church. Eight and one-half dozen chairs were ordered from Jones and Brothers.

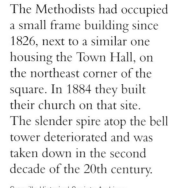

The Methodists had occupied a small frame building since 1826, next to a similar one housing the Town Hall, on the northeast corner of the square. In 1884 they built their church on that site. The slender spire atop the bell tower deteriorated and was taken down in the second decade of the 20th century.

Granville Historical Society Archives

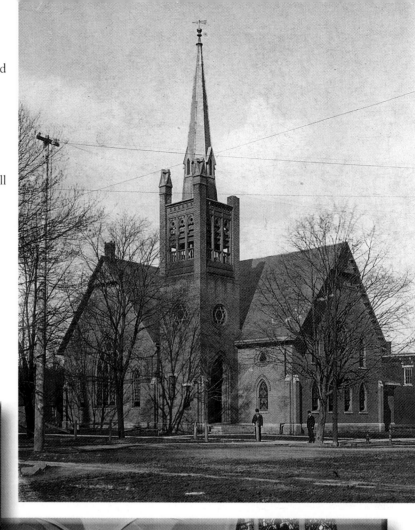

The congregation in the sanctuary of the Methodist Church in 1963.

Centenary United Methodist Church of Granville

Members of the congregation on the steps of St. Luke's, early in the twentieth century.

Granville Historical Society Archives

A Presbyterian Sunday School Class in 1881.

Granville Historical Society Archives

Religion was part of living in Granville.

William T. Utter leading a group of Methodists through the Old Colony Burying Ground to tell them about the early Methodists who are buried there.

Centenary United Methodist Church of Granville

In 1909 William Howard Doane funded the Fannie Doane Home for Missionary Children, named for his wife. House parents cared for children of overseas Baptist missionaries who were often out of the country for five years or more. The children were educated in the Granville schools and were part of the Granville community. After the Second World War, with vaccines available to make life safer for children in remote areas, need for the home decreased. It was closed in 1949 and remodeled into apartments for faculty at Denison University. In 1974, the building was no longer useful and was taken down. The site, at 518 West Broadway, is now occupied by condominiums.

Granville Historical Society Archives

Ruth and Harriet Jane Graham on the steps of Fannie Doane Home in 1933. They had been transferred from the Newton Center Home for Missionary Children in the summer of 1933. Their parents were in Chengtu, Szechuan Province, West China, and came home in 1948, just before the communist takeover. Both Ruth and Harriet Jane graduated from Granville High School.

Granville Historical Society Archives

Leslie Seagrave was crowned Queen of the May at Denison University in 1942. Both she and her brothers had lived in Fannie Doane Home while their parents were in Burma. Their father, Dr. Gordon Seagrave, was the famous "Burma Surgeon." He and his wife made their way home early in the 1940s after Burma was taken by Japanese forces. They had been away for five years.

Denison University Archives

(Left) The first chapel used by the Roman Catholic parish of St. Edward the Confessor, in a house on Broadway and Pearl. The site is now a parking lot for the Granville Inn. The parish of St. Edward the Confessor was established in 1946 when Bishop Michael J. Ready purchased the house at the northeast corner of Broadway and Pearl Streets. The parish first served thirty-five families. By 1954, a larger building was needed, and land was purchased at 785 Newark-Granville Road, where the church *(below)* was built. The parish continues to grow, and in 2004 a new edifice is under construction surrounding the 1954 building.

Church of St. Edward the Confessor

Elin Lisska's first communion at St. Edward the Confessor Church, 1983. Father Richard Lebarty was the celebrant of the Mass.

The Anthony Lisska Family

Pilgrim Evangelical Lutheran Church, associated with the Missouri Synod, first worshiped as a congregation December 25, 1954. The first meetings were in Recital Hall on the campus of Denison University, then in a house at 318 East College Street. They purchased a site at the southwest corner of West Broadway and Cherry Streets in 1964. The Education Building was erected in 1965 and used as sanctuary, classrooms, offices and a study for the pastor. In 1983, ground was broken for the church pictured above. The steeple was erected in 1984 *(top picture)*.

Granville Historical Society Archives

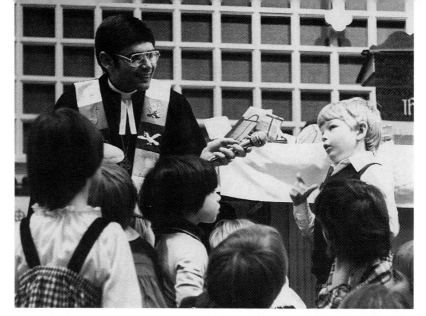

Presbyterian Pastor Steve Tischendorf lets little
Eric Evans explain the story, about 1975.

(Left, above ,and below)
First Presbyterian Church of Granville

Granville children happily participate in church activities.
This group poses in their finery at the front door of the
Presbyterian Church on a 1950s Easter Sunday.

Children of St. Luke's Episcopal
Church in 1993.

Granville Historical Society Archives

Karen Treece with
pre-school children at
the ecumenical vacation
bible school, June, 2004.

A Methodist group enjoys a picnic at the Whitehead farm about 1960.

Centenary United Methodist Church of Granville

In 1997 the parish of St. Edward celebrated its 50th anniversary with a parade and special Mass. A coverlet depicting their church commemorated the anniversary.

Church of St. Edward the Confessor

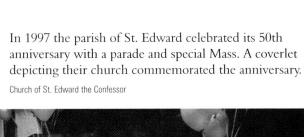

The congregation of the First Baptist Church beside the bus of relief supplies bound for Nicaragua, 1990.

First Baptist Church of Granville

Susan Potter, second from the right, leads the Presbyterian bell choir.

The Granville Sentinel

The Reverend George Williamson gives a boost to
a very young worker at the First Baptist Church's
Habitat for Humanity project in Newark.

The quilters of Centenary Methodist Church have provided warmth to many Granville citizens' homes.
The Granville Sentinel

Members of the First Baptist Church at the gay pride parade in Columbus, 1998.

(Above and top lef):
First Baptist Church of Granville

Some 600 pounds of food was collected by St. Luke's members
for the Food Pantry Network of Licking County in 2003.

St. Luke's Episcopal Church

The Church of
Jesus Christ of
Latter Day Saints,
2486 Newark-
Granville Road.

Kingdom Hall of Jehovah's
Witnesses, 2740 Newark-
Granville Road.

(Left and below)
Granville Historical Society Archives

The new Spring Hills Baptist
Church at 1820 Newark-
Granville Road. The Church
also operates a school, The
Granville Christian Academy.

Granville Village Planning Department

An ecumenical group prays for peace at the
peace pole on Broadway in downtown Granville.

The Granville Sentinel

On the anniversary of the
founding of the church, Pastor
Karen Chakoian and Associate
Pastor Thom Lamb beside the
memorial commemorating the
initial members of the church
formed in Massachusetts on
May 1, 1805.

First Presbyterian Church of Granville

Civil War Memorial for Company D, 113th Ohio Volunteer Infantry, known as "Granville's Own."

CHAPTER 7

Serving Home and Country

The twin ideals of patriotism and service are emblematic of Granville. The 1805 settlers included veterans of the Revolutionary War. In 1812 Jeremiah Munson recruited a company of Granville men under the command of Captain Levi Rose. Members of the Granville Band accompanied them, and the bassoon carried by that band is in the collections of the Granville Historical Society. During the Civil War, local enlistment quotas were oversubscribed and the casualties were a heavy burden. Men and women from the community have served in every war since that time. They nursed the wounded and fought in France during World War I, landed in Normandy, and fought in the Pacific Theatre in World War II. They served in Korea, in the jungles of Viet Nam, in the deserts of the middle-east, and in Afghanistan.

Granvillians also served their fellow citizens at home. Members of the Licking Company organized the immigration to Ohio and the fair division of property here. They built roads, established schools, organized and served in local government. Both then and now, they cared for their neighbors and others across the world, individually, and with philanthropies through churches, clubs, and other organizations.

William Gavit (1766-1854) a native of Groton,
Connecticut, sailed on "Privateers," civilian
vessels that harassed the British fleet during
the Revolutionary War. He was captured
several times, held in irons, and managed to
escape with harrowing experiences. He moved
to Granville, Massachusetts, with his family in
1788, joined the Licking Company in 1804,
and traveled with them to Ohio in 1805.
He became one of the pillars of the new
community and a pioneer in Methodism
in Ohio.

(All images on this page and facing page)
Granville Historical Society Archives

In 1813 Jeremiah Munson, one of Granville's early entrepreneurs, organized men to haul supplies to the troops engaging the British
on Lake Erie. This man was paid $32 to haul the baggage of forty recruits from Marietta to Zanesville, a distance of sixty miles.

This tintype of an unidentified Civil War soldier is typical of the images the soldiers sent home to their families. Photographers followed the troops and often did a brisk business in likenesses to send home.

This music book with hand written scores is titled: *"Used in the Army by L. H. Clouse 1865 for amusement 113 O.V.I."* He is listed as a fifer in Regimental records of Company D, and his comrades surely enjoyed the French Quadrille.

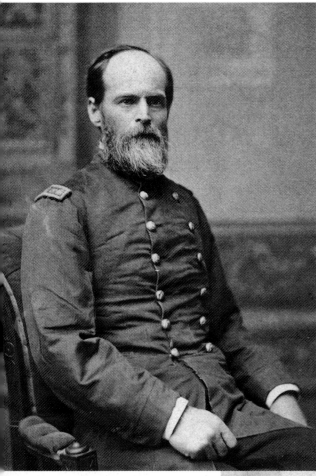

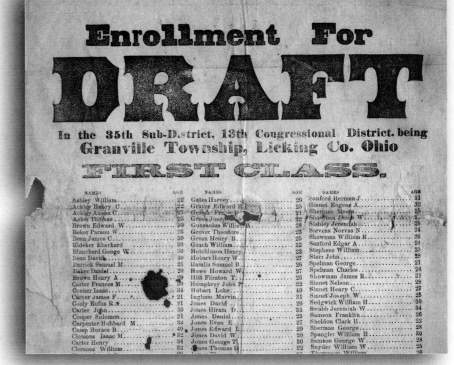

As the crisis at Fort Sumter was developing, Dr. Edwin Sinnett told his wife that if he was needed he must go with the troops. Some of the Granville boys had enlisted already and were in Company D of the 22nd O.V.I. under the command of Homer Thrall of Alexandria. The 76th Regiment was recruited in Licking County. Company D of the 113th O.V.I. was recruited by Marvin Munson in 1863 and was known as "Granville's Own." On February 9, 1863, Dr. Sinnett wrote to his wife from Nashville, " I had the good luck to see all of the 113th boys. They came in with the fleet on Saturday and I assure that it was a grand sight. . . The Regiment are all pretty well, some ten have been left at my hospital."

(All three images on this page)
Granville Historical Society Archives

A broadside listing the Granville Township men eligible for the draft for service in the Civil War. It was unnecessary to draft men in Granville Township because more Granville Township men volunteered than any other Township in Licking County. Patriotism and support for the Union ran high. The few "Copperheads" or "Peace Democrats" were pitied or worse. At the end of 1863, enlistments in Granville Township were 35 per cent above the quota. Utter remarks that "out of a total of about 3,000 men, women, and children, one eighth saw service and one eighth of those lost their lives."

Company D of the 22nd Ohio Volunteer Infantry. This seems to be a photograph of the unit in training camp.

William H. H. Avery's sword is in the collections of the Granville Historical Society, the gift of his great-great grandson, Thomas Avery.

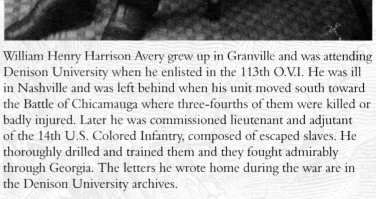

The embattled eagle from the cover of a Civil War songbook symbolizes the feelings in the country during the Civil War.

William Henry Harrison Avery grew up in Granville and was attending Denison University when he enlisted in the 113th O.V.I. He was ill in Nashville and was left behind when his unit moved south toward the Battle of Chicamauga where three-fourths of them were killed or badly injured. Later he was commissioned lieutenant and adjutant of the 14th U.S. Colored Infantry, composed of escaped slaves. He thoroughly drilled and trained them and they fought admirably through Georgia. The letters he wrote home during the war are in the Denison University archives.

Sgt. F. J. Cressy sent the sad news of the casualties at Chicamauga to Lt. Eno in Granville on a carefully folded piece of brown wrapping paper, now preserved in the Granville Historical Society archives. Company D had left home a year before. Of the forty-seven men who went into battle, only eleven came though without harm. Eight were killed and several others died of their wounds.

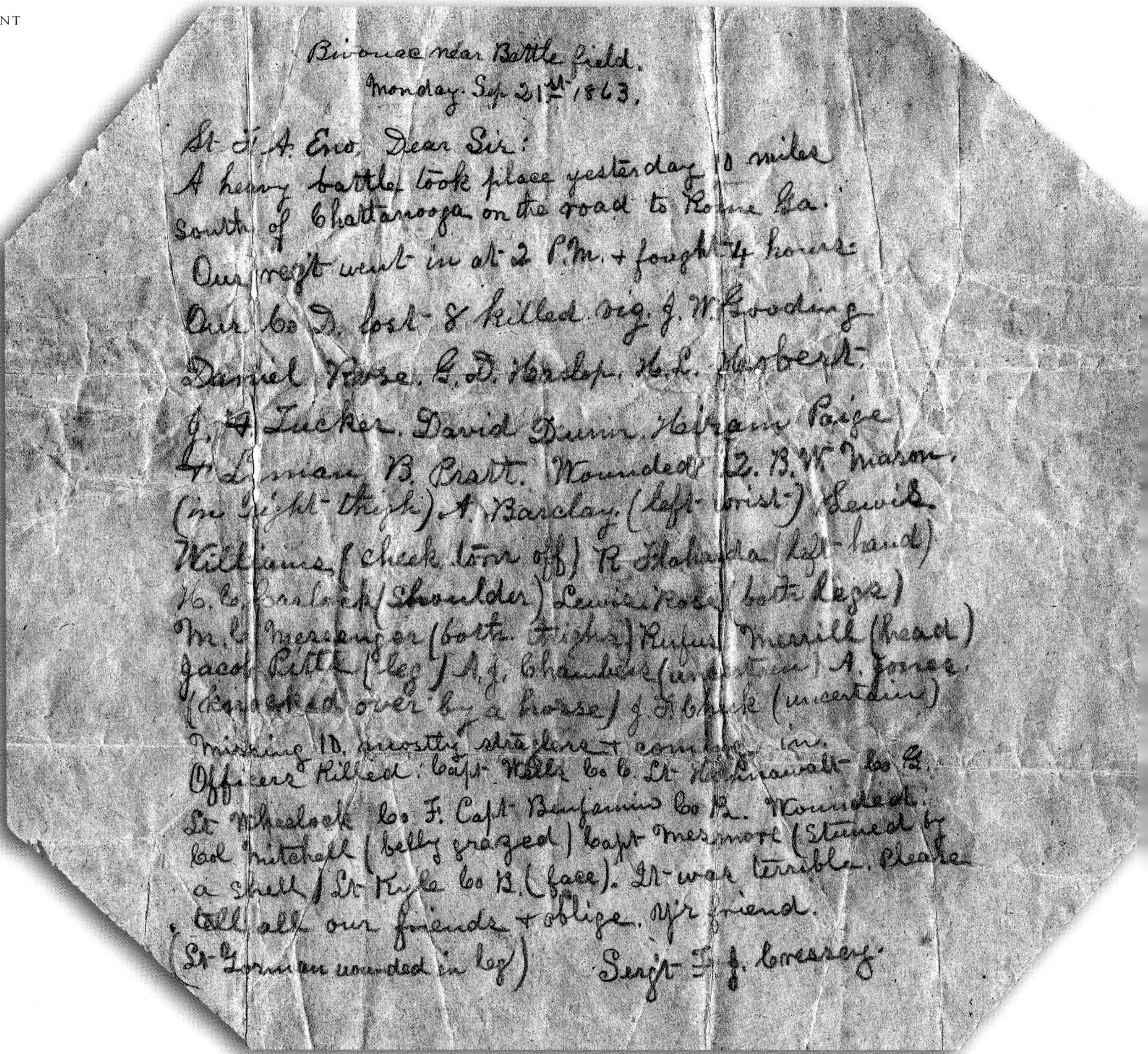

(All images on this page and facing page)
Granville Historical Society Archives

Bivouac near Battle field.
Monday. Sep 21st 1863.

Lt. F. A. Eno, Dear Sir:
A heavy battle took place yesterday 10 miles
south of Chattanooga on the road to Rome Ga.
Our regt went in at 2 P.M. + fought 4 hours.
Our Co D. lost 8 killed viz. J. W. Gooding
Daniel [illegible]. G. D. [illegible]. H. L. [illegible].
J. A. Tucker. David Dunn. Hiram Paige
L. Lorman B. Pratt. Wounded Lt. B. W. Mason
(in right thigh) A. Barclay (left wrist) Lewis
Williams (cheek torn off) R. [illegible] (left hand)
H. C. [illegible] (shoulder) Lewis Ross (both legs)
M. C. Messenger (both thighs) Rufus Merrill (head)
Jacob Pitts (leg) A. J. Chambers ([illegible]) A. Jones.
(knocked over by a horse) J. F. Chick (uncertain)
Missing 10. mostly stragglers + coming in.
Officers Killed: Capt Wells Co C. Lt [illegible] Co G.
Lt Wheelock Co F. Capt Benjamin Co B. Wounded.
Col Mitchell (belly grazed) Capt Mesmore (Stunned by
a shell) Lt Kyle Co B. (face). It was terrible. Please
tell all our friends + oblige. Yr friend.
(Lt Gorman wounded in leg) Sergt F. J. Cressey.

First Lieutenant Charles Sinnett's commission dated June 9, 1864, in Chattanooga, Tennessee.

Charles Sinnett, the younger brother of Dr. Edwin Sinnett, was elected by his men as a lieutenant in Company D, 113th O.V.I., when the unit was in Louisville on their way south. After the war he estimated that about 300 men from Licking County served in the war and that thirty-seven lost their lives and that eleven more died shortly after returning home.

HEAD-QUARTERS DEPARTMENT OF THE CUMBERLAND.

Chattanooga, Tenn., June 9th, 1864.

Lieut

The General Commanding intends to recommend you to the President of the United States as a suitable person to receive the commission of *1st Lieutenant* in the Veteran Volunteer Engineer regiment to be raised from the Army of the Cumberland, in accordance with the provisions of the Act of Congress, passed May 18th, 1864.

You will immediately notify this Office of your acceptance or non-acceptance of the commission hereby tendered to you. If no reply is received by the *12* of *June* you will be considered as having declined the nomination and the place will be filled by another appointment.

By Command of Major-General Thomas.

Wm M Michael
Assistant Adjutant General.

To *Lieut Charles Sinnett*
113 O.V. Infy
Hd Quarters Pioneer Bry
Chattanooga Tenn

Veterans of the Civil War gathered in front of the Baptist Church for a portrait in 1888. From the left, in the back row: Jackson, Kidd, La Ferre, Willams, Weston, Griffing, Kelvey, Schwab, Sinnett. Seated: Hayes, Frederick, Samson, Church, DeBow, Warman, Malone. In front: Jones, Gregory, Harmon, Brubaker, Evans.

The World War I Gold Star Mothers join the Blue Star mothers beside the Baptist Church. The blue star signified a son in military service. The gold star announced that the service man had given his life for his country.

Granville Historical Society Archives

Private Frank James served in Company L, 138th Infantry Division, in France during World War I. He was a twenty-six year old farmer when he enlisted in Granville in 1918.

James Family, courtesy of Ruth Burgoon

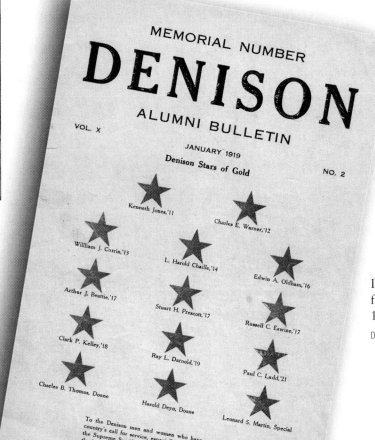

MEMORIAL NUMBER

DENISON

ALUMNI BULLETIN

VOL. X

JANUARY 1919

Denison Stars of Gold

NO. 2

Kenneth Jones, '11

Charles E. Warner, '12

William J. Currin, '13

L. Harold Chaille, '14

Edwin A. Oldham, '16

Arthur J. Beattie, '17

Stuart H. Prescott, '17

Russell C. Eswine, '17

Clark P. Kelley, '18

Ray L. Darnold, '19

Paul C. Ladd, '21

Charles B. Thomas, Doane

Harold Deyo, Doane

Leonard S. Martin, Special

To the Denison men and women who have answered our country's call for service, especially to those who have made the Supreme Sacrifice, whether in cantonment, camp or on the battle field, this number of the Denison Alumni B is affectionately ins

Denison University honored its fallen students in the January 1919 Alumni Bulletin.

Denison University Archives

Granville women rallied to support French soldiers before the United States entered the first World War. They formed a unit of the American Fund for the French Wounded. The secretary, Marguarite McCollom, reported that the packing and shipping committee had sent 55 cases since October 12, 1916. Included were such items as 1,528 comfort pillows, 370 pairs of pajamas, 74 pairs of slippers, 23 yards of gauze, and 42 Victrola records.

(All three images)
Granville Historical Society Archives

Armistice Day was an important holiday, up through the second World War. It was always observed with a minute of silence at 11:00 AM.

"Lest We Forget"

ARMISTICE DAY SERVICES

held under the auspices of

The American Legion, Granville Business Men's Association and Citizens of Granville.

Monday, November 11, 1929.   3:00 P.M.

Granville women, some dressed as Red Cross nurses, join the 1918 Armistice Day parade.

V-12 Marines parade down Chapel Walk. After Pearl Harbor on December 7, 1941, most Denison men, both faculty and students, were drafted or enlisted in the armed services. To partly fill the void, service groups trained at Denison during the war years; first, a Pre-Meteorological Group, then V-12 and V-5 units of Marine Corps and Navy. The women students moved to Fraternity Row, the service units to the dormitories. The annual calendar was completely re-arranged to military specifications.

Dean Cyril Richards decided that the Denison men in service should have news of their college while they were serving their country. On March 25, 1942, he dictated a letter to be mimeographed and sent to those for whom he had addresses. He described some of the changes that had come to Denison and asked service men to send their current address, rank, and some personal reactions—and they did. He published quotations from the reactions in subsequent editions. Newsletter No. 30, May 15, 1946, was sent to 1,850 Denison men and women. It listed the names of 52 Denisonians who had died for their country. The thirty letters Cy Richards sent to Denison service men and women cover more that 550 pages. They are preserved in the Denison University Archives and are a remarkable record of their reactions to the war.

(Both images)
Denison University Archives

Lt. H. Maclain (Mac) Burriss was a pilot stationed at a forward outpost on a Pacific island during the war. He wrote to his friend Phil Oxley, who was also in the Pacific Theater, and told of being shot down by several Zeros. He was able to get out and "set off in my little rubber yacht, undoubtedly the most lonesome boy you ever saw." An American PBY rescued him that afternoon. He told Phil that he had just flown again and had downed four Japanese Zeros. The following day he went up again and was shot down and lost.

Denison University Archives

Lloyd Philipps trained at Ft. McClellan, Alabama in 1943. He landed with the allied troops at Normandy and fought in France.

Lloyd Philipps Family

Rolan Thompson, with his camera, in the Army Air Corps during World War II. Well known in Granville after the war as a photographer, his studio was on Broadway.

Thompson Family, courtesy of Lee Biciunas

Leroy "Ace" Morgan served in Europe. He wrote, "Granville used to be so close and the war so remote—now things are just reversed, with Granville almost a dream of the way people should live after the war is finished. The Army is probably the finest accredited university in the world, possessing excellent departments in Disillusionment, Discouragement, and Humility. . . Many have written of how sorry they were to leave Granville. I am thankful I had to go away. Without ever having been away I might not have known how much I wanted to go back." Ace did not come back; the Denison Theatre Workshop is named in his memory.

Denison University Archives

With men off to fight, local farmers had to look for additional help to harvest crops. Margaret Richards and her friend Jeanette Marlow volunteered to pick apples for a local orchard.

To show support and to provide a place to relax, the community, with support from Denison and the Salvation Army, helped establish the Red Shield Canteen in the lower level of the Opera House in 1943. Granville women baked cookies and young women were eager to sign up for shifts to talk with the service men.

(All three images)
Denison University Archives

New fabric was scarce and sailors stationed at Denison helped the girls with an old clothing drive.

Seamen entering the Chapel in June 1945 for the recognition service on completion of their course at Denison.

Denison University Archives

Lloyd "Bud" Philipps, Jr., served in the Mediterranean from 1967 to 1972, including two tours on the aircraft carrier USS *Saratoga*.

Lloyd Philipps Family

Veterans who had returned to college pictured on V-E day, May 8, 1945.

Denison University Archives

Service to the Granville community began with the Licking Company members who organized the move to Ohio and conducted the auction to divide the land equitably. Granvillians have worked for the common good since that time. Service on Township and Village Boards depends on volunteers and is largely unpaid.

The Granville Village Council in June 1952. From the left: Harry Pierce, Robert Dixon, Leslie Major, Fred Eisle, Gene Wolford, Richard Howe.

A town meeting at the Opera House in 1954. Seated at the table are Mayor John Bjelke and Clerk Carl Frazier. "Doc" Rohrer is seated at center. William Utter is in the second row and Dick Mahard at the far right.

(Both images)
Granville Historical Society Archives

Before streets were paved in the second decade of the twentieth century, dust was a problem for pedestrians and housewives. The Village allayed this by sending out the water wagon during dry periods.

(All three images)
Granville Historical Society Archives

Laying water lines on Broadway, 1885. Pollution of shallow wells and the danger of fire led to the establishment of the modern water system in Granville. Voters approved construction of a deep well southwest of the Village, the water to be pumped to a 93,000 gallon reservoir on College Hill, to flow by gravity to village spigots. Professor J. L. Gilpatrick, Crayton W. Black and Charles W. Bryant were elected water works trustees. The College granted right of way for the water lines and Professor Gilpatrick's surveying class determined the slope of the streets. Water shot over the roof of a three-storey building during the test on November 6, 1885.

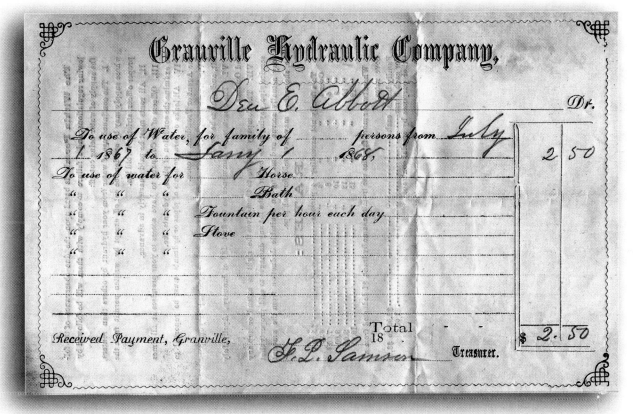

Deacon Elizur Abbott paid the Granville Hydraulic Company $2.50 for water from July through December 1867. In 1854, the Hydraulic Company ran lines from a spring near the Everett property on Lower Louden Street two miles to a reservoir at the base of Sugar Loaf. Water was supplied to the Granville Female Seminary and to several homes at the west end of Granville. Expense and frequent repair of the tile pipes led to the gradual demise of the company.

The Granville water pumping station, about 1910.

(Top and bottom right)
Granville Historical Society Archives

Laying a sewer line on Newark Granville Road. Modern equipment makes this job easier than in 1885.

The Granville Sentinel

Repairing the gas line at Main and Elm Streets.

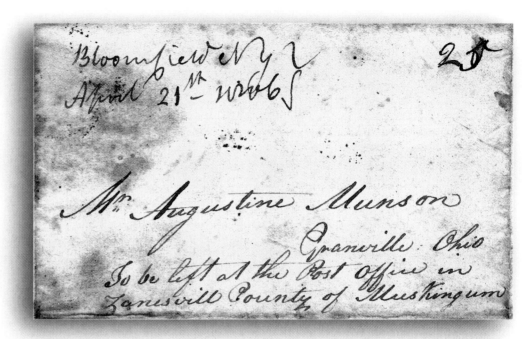

When the 1805 settlers left Zanesville they passed beyond the limit of the United States Postal Service and the last semblance of roads. They left their names at the Zanesville Post Office so that mail could be held for them. Someone rode back to get Augustine Munson's letter and the other mail for Granville.

Since 1979 Gary Hamilton has carried the mail in Granville.

The Granville Sentinel

"Mr. Lake brought the mail, snow or rain." Dependable mail delivery on Centerville Street in the early 20th century.

(Above and top)
Granville Historical Society Archives

On October 16, 1882, the Midland Telephone Company installed a telephone in Bryant's Drug Store, the first in the village. Someone was sent with a written message when a call was received. Blanche Horton, Granville's "Central," is pictured in the Granville exchange in 1936, when the new telephone building opened on Broadway. She retired in 1942 after 42 years of service.

Granville Historical Society Archives

Hospital Twig 19's book sale was an annual event in Granville. A young reader tries an interesting book while others browse.

The Granville Sentinel

The Denison staff for buildings, grounds and maintenance gathered on December 15, 1948, for a group portrait at the Denison Heating Plant on South Main Street.

Richard Horton

Helen Dunfield was instrumental in establishing the Granville Fellowship, for Granville's senior citizens, in Sinnett House. The house had been Clara Sinnett White's girlhood home, and she had it moved to the rear of the lot when the Library was built in 1924. In 2004, the Library needed space for expansion and the Fellowship moved to new quarters in the Board of Education building on Granger Street.

Anestis Diakopoulos, used with permission

H. E. "Happy" Lamson, Roe Morrow, and J. W. "Doc" Rohrer with the old hose reel used by the village until after the fire that burned the shops on the south side of Broadway in 1927.

(Above and bottom right)
Granville Historical Society Archives

The volunteer firemen stand with their ladder truck outside their garage in the back of the village hall on south Main Street, about 1930.

Granville Life-Style Museum

Denison students have been members of the Granville Volunteer Fire Department for many years. These students served in 1988.

Denison students volunteer for many activities organized by the Denison Community Association. Two women at work on a house for Habitat for Humanity.

Denison University Archives

Buckets hanging from Maple trees were a common sight in February. Fearful of damaging the Village trees, the Kiwanis Club now taps trees on woodlots in the Township and boils down the sap in their sugar house.

Granville Historical Society Archives

Kiwanis member Dale Gleason serves the pancakes at the annual March breakfast featuring Granville Maple Syrup in 1998.

The Granville Sentinel

The Granville Rotary Club sponsors Operation Smile, championed by Doug Barno, to make a difference in childrens' lives by correcting facial deformities.

(All three images)
The Granville Sentinel

High School students are eager to volunteer for many causes. These students conducted a food drive in the early 1990s.

Mary Ellen Everett at the Granville Recycling Center on South Main, about 1980. The dwindling number of volunteers forced the Center to close after several years. In 2004, with the cooperation of Denison University, a new Recycling Facility opened on North Street.

The centennial logo on one of the souvenirs. A "vest pocket mirror" is on the reverse side. The price was ten cents.

(Both images)
Granville Historical Society Archives

GRANVILLE
1805
GRANVILLE OHIO. SEPT. 1905
1905
CENTENNIAL

The centennial parade, September 7, 1905.

CHAPTER 8

Celebrations

The 75th anniversary of the Granville community in 1880 was celebrated with speeches, reminiscences, and an exhibit of "relics of pioneers." These were collected and led to the formation of the Granville, Ohio, Historical Society in 1885. Granville's centennial in September 1905 was the largest and most elaborate celebration ever held in the community. More than 100 persons served on committees. The speakers for the programs read like a *Who's Who* in Granville history. The Governor of Ohio, other prominent government officials, and college and university presidents attended. Many former residents returned, and class reunions were held. Flags flew over Broadway, and all important buildings were draped with bunting. Formal programs were presented on eight consecutive days. There were several processions and a major parade on September 7th, "Granville Day." Picnics, teas, and receptions occurred almost daily. A special Granville edition of *The Old Northwest Genealogical Quarterly* with 435 pages was compiled and published. Its lists of church members, students in the various schools, and burials in the community cemeteries are an invaluable resource today. The legacy of the centennial lived on in monuments, publications, collections, and most importantly in community spirit.

Granville's 100th Anniversary

St. Luke's Episcopal Church with its handsome centennial bunting.

The Opera House was centennial headquarters.

(All images on this page and facing page)
Granville Historical Society Archives

The Buxton Inn decorated for the centennial.

A covered wagon in the centennial parade symbolized the 1805 migration.

The official envelope displayed a variation of the centennial logo.

The grounds of the Old Granville Female College building were crowded with families and friends of the Welsh settlers of Granville Township on Homecomers' Day, September 8th. Just visible is the Welsh dragon emblem over the porch at right center.

The program for the Welsh reunion and musical festival, Friday September 8, 1905.

(All three images)
Granville Historical Society Archives

The centennial letterhead listed the major officers and committees.

The large glacial boulder on top of Sugar Loaf is a legacy of Granville's centennial. It was unveiled on Founder's Day, November 17, 1905, the 100th anniversary of the pioneer's first worship service on the town plat around the felled beech tree. The memorial was the gift of Mary Case Minton who is seen here with her family. Pictured, from the left, her husband, J.V. Minton, Dora Howland Case, Ed F. Hobart, Mary Case Minton, her brother Burton Case, and her sister Helen Case Hobart. The monument was given in memory of Mary Case Williams, daughter of Captain Levi Rose and Polly Stowe Rose. The family composed the inscription on the bronze plaque which reads: "In grateful remembrance of the members of the Licking Land Company who came from Granville, Massachusetts, and founded this town in the wilderness November 17, 1805. They builded better than they knew. To God be the glory forever and ever. Amen."

Granville's 125th Anniversary

The Welsh Hills Grange and the Granville Grange co-operated on a float, drawn by a handsome team of horses, for the 125th anniversary parade.

In 1930, the community celebrated the 125th anniversary of Granville. It began with a grand parade down Broadway.

(All three images)
Granville Historical Society Archives

Several leading citizens served as the executive committee for the 125th anniversary. *Left to right:* Ruth Sharer Marlow, Ed Jones, Clara Sinnett White, Dr. J. W. Rohrer, Dora Case, Wat Thomas.

During the 125th anniversary celebration, the gymnasium in Cleveland Hall on the Denison campus was turned into exhibit space for the history of Granville and its institutions. This section had artifacts and memorabilia from the Granville Female College (1829–1898). Some of the items displayed were lent for the occasion by families. A few were given to the Granville Historical Society, including the little white chair and the school bench and desk on the floor at the left of the picture.

Granville Historical Society Archives

Granville's 150th Anniversary

Fullers Market delivery jeep pulled their float in the Sesquicentennial Parade.

Dramatic scenes from Granville's past, written by Denison English Professors Paul L. Bennett and Nancy E. Lewis, were performed at several locations in town. Here is the re-enactment of workmen at the Reverend Ahab Jinks new home laying bricks on the Sabbath. He was anxious to finish before the first frost and convinced his contractor, Lucius Mower, that it was a "a work of necessity." The resulting furor over violating the Sabbath led to a split in the Congregational Church.

The band that led guests between the historic scenes in September 1955. Conducted by Denison Music Professor George Hunter, it had two flutes, two clarinets, one bass clarinet, and a drum.

(Two top images and bottom left)
Granville Historical Society Archives

Another scene depicts Granville men leaving for the California gold fields in 1849. Anxious families and the Reverend Jacob Little, at the right, see them off.

Denison University Archives

Governor Lausche turned the key to open the new Granville Historical Society Museum, dedicated on September 30, 1955, the first day of Granville's Sesquicentennial Celebration. Shown, from the left: Hayesel Huston Eaton; William T. Utter, historian and author; Governor Frank Lausche; Henry Eaton, president of the society; Mrs. Lausche; and Alma Utter.

The renovation and enlargement of this 1815 building was made possible by a bequest from Clara Sinnett White. Charles Webster Bryant had hoped and planned for a museum devoted to Granville's history in 1885. Marvin Munson, Charles B. White, and Francis Shepardson published articles in *The Granville Times*, about this need. The possessions of the Society, which had been stored in various places over the years, were brought together under one roof for the first time in 1955. Constructed as a bank for the Alexandrian Society the building had been used as a store, restaurant, barber shop, and interurban depot, before being restored for the Museum.

(Both images)
Granville Historical Society Archives

Independence Day

The Fourth of July is Granville's signature holiday today, with the Mile Long Parade, a carnival, bands, dances, athletic contests, picnics, and family and class reunions. During most of the nineteenth century the observance included a band, a patriotic oration, and a dinner. In 1828, Captain Spelman's company of infantry, accompanied by a full band, marched to an open field. After the Declaration of Independence was read, an "elegant" oration was delivered. A table twelve rods long was required for the dinner. The editor of *The Wanderer* noted that he was highly gratified with the decent behavior of all present.

In the 1914 July 4th parade Ed Evans advertised his plumbing business with a bathtub and kitchen sink on his float.

(All three images)
Granville Historical Society Archives

The Buxton Jewelry float and a band passing the Methodist Church in the 1915 parade.

Float with the Y. M. C. A. and other groups in an Independence Day parade in the 1920s.

In 1914 the float for the Daughters of the American Revolution followed the wagon for Bash the Ice Man, past the businesses on the north side of Broadway.

A young spectator perched on an automobile watches the "Own Room Club" float pass the Avery-Downer house in the 1920s.

(All three images)
Granville Historical Society Archives

The Fourth of July in 1917 included a carnival and lighted standards on Prospect Street to celebrate the completion of the first phase of downtown street paving.

Old time fire fighting equipment rounds the corner at Plum Street to go east on Broadway in July 1956. Spectators had not spread to this end of Broadway, as they do today. The row of graceful old elm trees fronting Denison's lower campus were planted by Charles Sawyer 120 years earlier.

(Right and bottom left)
Sidney Hollingworth, courtesy of Florence Hollingworth Wright

"Happy Birthday U. S. A." on West Broadway in 1949.

Lifeguards and swimmers rode on the Spring Valley float, about 1969.

Roberts Family, courtesy of Anne Ormond

Beth, Shawn, and Rosalie Hoover won the prize for the best costumes in the children's division of the Fourth of July Parade in the early 1960s. Shawn carried the sword that his great-grandfather carried in the Civil War.

Gloria Hoover, used with permission

Ned Wright waves from a swinging chair during the Fourth of July carnival in 1959.

Sidney Hollingworth, courtesy of Florence Hollingworth Wright

A clown entertains the crowd. Often they distribute candy.

(Both images)
Granville Historical Society Archives

Neighborhood floats are a tradition.

In recent years, the Granville Kiwanis Club has organized the Fourth of July Celebration. Club members take care of set-up and tear-down and they even dispense food to the hungry crowd.

Centenary United Methodist Church of Granville

The horns of the Granville High School band. The band has been a popular feature of the parade for many years.

(Above and bottom left)
Granville Historical Society Archives

The American Legion color guard leading the parade.

Viaduct Opening, 1929

The John Sutphen Jones Memorial Viaduct, which soared over Raccoon Creek and the railroad in a graceful curve, was opened with a grand celebration presided over by Ohio Governor Myers Y. Cooper on November 26, 1929.

A color guard and dignitaries preceded the band during the opening ceremonies for the John Sutphen Jones Memorial Viaduct.

(All three images)
Granville Historical Society Archives

A gun salute in honor of Governor Cooper opened the festivities.

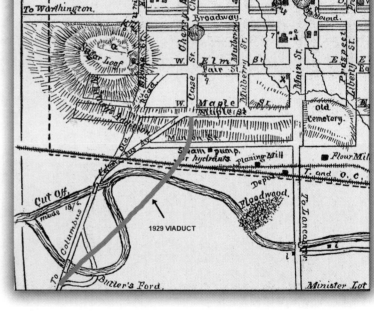

Before 1929, the road to Columbus angled southwest from the corner of Cherry and Maple Streets, descended a steep hill, and crossed Raccoon Creek near the site of the water plant, more than a block west of the present Cherry Street–Route 16 crossing. The old road was subject to floods in the valley and was a steep climb to the Village for horses and later for motor vehicles. The new level viaduct, indicated by a solid line on the above map, started just south of Maple Street and joined the Columbus Road south of Raccoon Creek.

A 1900 "curved dash" Oldsmobile and a high-wheel bicycle parade past the Broadway businesses. The tracks in the street were for the interurban cars.

Virginia Jones cut the ribbon to open the viaduct memorializing her father who had died in 1927. Governor Cooper is beside her in the dark coat and hat.

The Viaduct in 1955. Sidney Hollingworth, courtesy of Florence Hollingworth Wright

The new Jones Memorial Viaduct in 1929.

(Above, top left, and top right)
Granville Historical Society Archives

. . . and any excuse!

Granville citizens are always eager to celebrate a holiday; an important one in the early twentieth century was George Washington's Birthday. The Denison students chose a couple to portray George and Martha, and an elaborate dinner was served.

On George Washington's Birthday in 1915, the Denison students' exuberant celebration spread to downtown Granville.

Denison University Archives

Florence Hollingworth is ready for the Harvest Festival in 1941.

Sidney Hollingworth,
courtesy of Florence Hollingworth Wright

Little ghosts, goblins, witches, and skeletons roam the sidewalks before Halloween.

The Granville Sentinel

Christmas Candlelight Walking Tour

"A Granville Gift To Families"
Saturday, December 5, 1998 • 6:00 p.m. to 9:00 p.m.

Sponsored by Granville Business & Professional Association, Granville, Ohio

The Granville Business and Professional Association became the Granville Chamber of Commerce in 2001, but they continued to sponsor the annual Holiday Walking Tour in downtown Granville. The tour signals the beginning of the holiday season. All the local businesses are open with seasonal decorations. A program of musical events is held in each church, Burke Hall on the Denison campus, and in the museums. Santa Claus waits for children's requests. Hundreds of people fill the streets and walk from site to site.

Luminaria line the streets and the walks to each church, business, or museum.

(Above and top)
Granville Historical Society Archives

A very special celebration in Granville occurred in 2002. Lea Ann Parsley was given a hero's welcome and parade when she returned home from the Olympic Winter Games with the Silver Medal in the Skeleton race. Here she waves to the excited crowd during her parade. All Granville rejoiced with her.

The Granville Sentinel

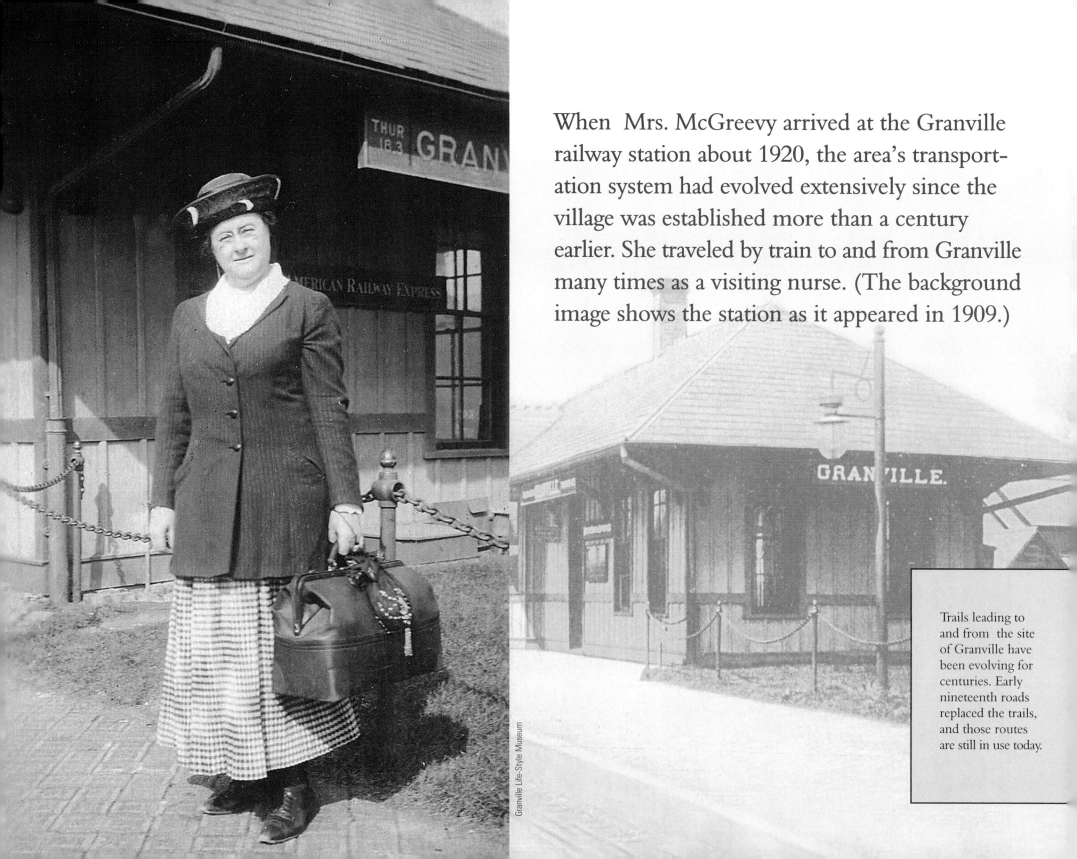

When Mrs. McGreevy arrived at the Granville railway station about 1920, the area's transportation system had evolved extensively since the village was established more than a century earlier. She traveled by train to and from Granville many times as a visiting nurse. (The background image shows the station as it appeared in 1909.)

Trails leading to and from the site of Granville have been evolving for centuries. Early nineteenth roads replaced the trails, and those routes are still in use today.

CHAPTER 9

Comings and Goings

embers of the Licking Company came to Granville in 1805 by ox-drawn wagons and horseback. Earlier inhabitants had come and gone on foot, leaving trails and impressive mounds. The 1805 immigrant group gathered at a squatters cabin east of the present Village, before coming on to the town plat as a group. After choosing lots and farms, the settlers discussed highways at their first meeting and appointed a committee to open roads to Lancaster, Worthington, and Owl Creek (now Mt. Vernon). New settlers arrived, a few men went back east for their families, and a few just moved on. People have been coming here to live, going from this place for short or long visits elsewhere, or moving to different places ever since.

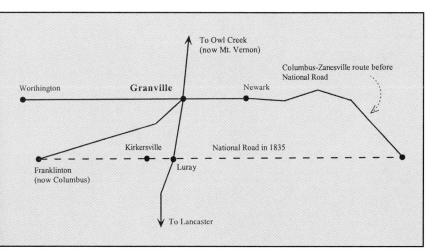

To Owl Creek (now Mt. Vernon)

Columbus-Zanesville route before National Road

Worthington   **Granville**   Newark

Kirkersville   National Road in 1835

Franklinton (now Columbus)   Luray

To Lancaster

163

Elizabeth Hubbard recorded a word picture of her trip to Granville from New England in 1834. She and her sister Joanna traveled from Cleveland on the Ohio Canal:

"We embarked about 3 P.M.; were not long in examining our premises. In the stern of the boat were two small cabins—the inner of these were exclusively the ladies' apartment. It had three pretended double berths on each side & a place big enough for two to stand abreast between them. The outer room is used as a sittng room by day & a dormitory (both for gent & ladies) by night. On each side, two long boxes covered with cushions answered the treble purpose of settees beds and drawers. Over these boxes, framed sacking was hung at night to add to the number of berths: making in all eight beds in this cabin. But the closeness of the air at night & sundry other things rendered the idea of bed time revolting. Our meals were truly sickening. It was a great comfort to find one article clean & good, which the crackers usually were. The heterogeneous particles of matter often observable in the milk & water made drinking very unplesant. We did not express our disagreeable sensations on this point until after we left the boat. . . . We passed from Cleaveland to Akron, 38 miles, in 23 hours. Passed 44 locks, 15 of these occur in the two sections directly north of Akron."

Denison University Archives

Suddenly it was possible to ship and receive goods between Granville and the East Coast.

Advertisement:
The Granville Intelligencer

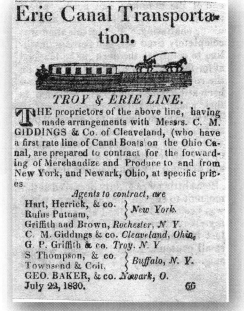

Showman's Arch, built as an aqueduct for the Granville Feeder Canal in 1832, today carries Cherry Valley Road over Raccoon Creek.

Granville Historical Society Archives

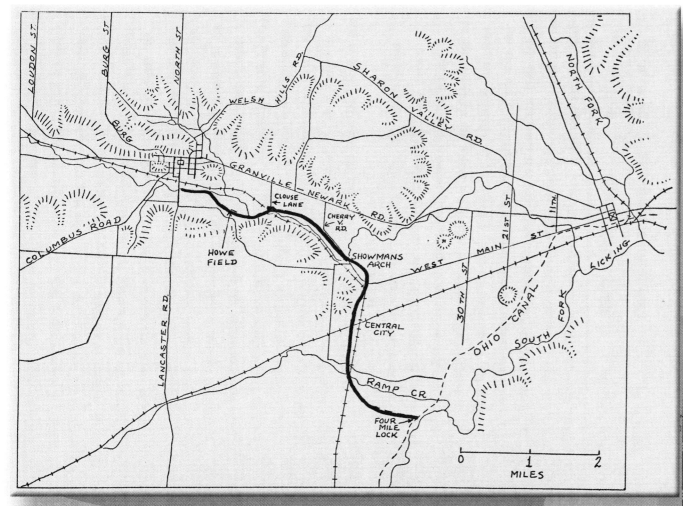

A sketch map by Albert W. Davison, Jr., showing the route of the Granville Feeder Canal, completed in 1832, and its connection to the Ohio-Erie Canal.

Canal Society of Ohio

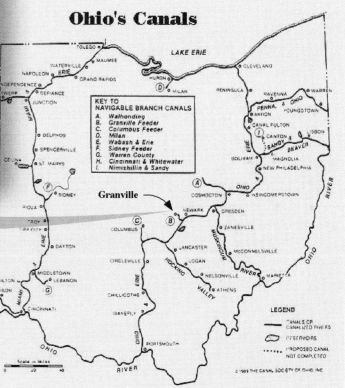

Harry Ellis Thomas and his father, who farmed on the Worthington Road, determined to go to California to look for gold in 1850. They embarked from New York with about sixteen of their neighbors and crossed the Isthmus of Panama on foot. From there they set sail for "Kally Phorny" with a ship captain who became deranged and finally committed suicide. A second ship delivered them safely to San Francisco. They mined near Sacramento for 18 months, returning home with a modest amount of gold. The following is an extract from a letter home dated May 12, 1851 (the original spelling is preserved):

"Altho wee have done beter than the average of miners in California since we have bin here. Thir is 8 partners of us working together. wee are working with a Machien caled A long Tom it is about 58 feete long and the troves are about 18 inches wide at the head and 4 feete wide at the lower end wee have A riddle at the lower end with lets the dirt gold and small gravel stones gow through into a box. . . Wee can employ 15 or 20 men with work at our Machien. . . Their was twelve of us at work last week a diging arais to Drean

HO BOYS! FOR CALIFONIA!!

ANY one who is really anxious to join a company to emigrate to California, and has *right good grit*, will please call at the Post Office and make himself known within a few days! Come on ye Granvillians. *Now is the time.*
Granville January 3d, 1849.

the water of from our Claims, and wee washed the dirt through our Tom wee took oupt in four days $582 dolars . . . The general average of the miners around whare wee are is not over 4 or 5 dolars per day"

Ellen Hayes' grandfather, Horace Wollcott, lived in this farm house across the road from The Tannery operated by her father. The house, known as Spring Hill, was later owned by the Futerer and Ackley families. The site at 530 Newark-Granville Road, beside the east slope of Mt. Parnassus, is now occupied by an office park. Ellen Hayes, describes her grandfather's feelings about going west:

Granville Historical Society Archives

"His paper was usually the New York Tribune, Greeley's Tribune, established in 1841. Grandfather was probably one of the early subscribers. The writings of the great editor suited him: he believed in the far west to which young men were editorially exhorted to go. Good judgment and perhaps some sense of duty must have influenced him to 'stay by the stuff'—the little Ohio farm which had so long claimed his care and rewarded his skill; otherwise he would have been off to the Missouri country which was then 'out west.' He contented himself with outfitting his boys one after another. I recall one morning when a team of valuable horses with a trim new moving-wagon stood at the big gate by the spring. There were some sheep; horses and sheep were headed west. Grandfather had thought of everything for the journey and for the new home beyond the Mississippi. His pioneer heart must have stirred with longing for a share of his son's adventure; but he turned with silent resignation to his days in the familiar fields 'round the hill and his evenings with the Tribune."

—Ellen Hayes, *Wild Turkeys and Tallow Candles*

Fletcher O. Marsh was a mainstay of Denison in the mid 19th century as Professor of Mathematics, Treasurer, and Secretary of the Board of Trustees. His wife recalled their arrival in Granville in 1853 when the College was still situated on Columbus Road, southwest of town:

"We arrived in Granville early in the evening of November 20th, 1853. The stage from Newark left us at the Hotel, kept, I think, by Levi Rose, on the corner opposite the Bank, same (north) side of the street. The President, Dr. Hall, met us there with his buggy and as he was a large man, it was with some difficulty that we piled in, I with our baby Ella, five months old, and satchels and bundles in abundance. The night was fearfully dark and Oh! Such a road to the College Farm. I was sure that we should be tipped into the mud and the mile and a half seemed like five miles. Happy was I when we turned into a big gate and saw the light from the windows. Father [F. O. Marsh] . . . supplied the pulpit all winter . . . receiving $ 5.00 per Sunday, he held nightly meetings for three weeks and visited every family in the Church. Nights he would walk home, part of the way on a fence as the creek would overflow the road."

—Denison University, *Marsh Papers*

1. Original site for the college
2. Tannery House

William T. Utter, *Granville The Story of An Ohio Village* © 1956

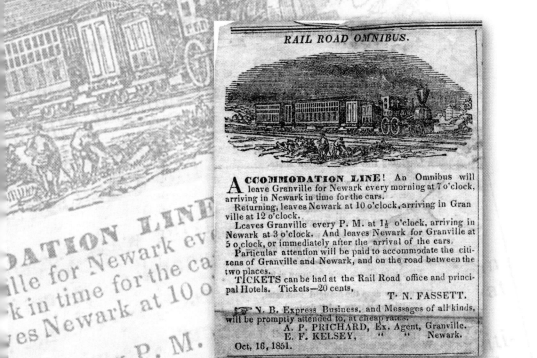

RAIL ROAD OMNIBUS.

ACCOMMODATION LINE! An Omnibus will leave Granville for Newark every morning at 7 o'clock, arriving in Newark in time for the cars.

Returning, leaves Newark at 10 o'clock, arriving in Granville at 12 o'clock.

Leaves Granville every P. M. at 1½ o'clock, arriving in Newark at 3 o'clock. And leaves Newark for Granville at 5 o'clock, or immediately after the arrival of the cars.

Particular attention will be paid to accommodate the citizens of Granville and Newark, and on the road between the two places.

TICKETS can be had at the Rail Road office and principal Hotels. Tickets—20 cents,

T· N. FASSETT.

N. B. Express Business, and Messages of all kinds, will be promptly attended to, at cheap rates.

A. P. PRICHARD, Ex. Agent, Granville.
E. F. KELSEY, " " Newark.

Oct. 16, 1851.

Granville Historical Society Archives

"Granville's public connection with Newark was an omnibus, a four-horse lumbering vehicle which began running in 1849. We who dwelt by Clear Run could hear this omnibus as it rounded the shoulder of the big hill: it came clattering down the road and over the stone bridge and disappeared from sight behind the next high ground, rumbling and creaking as it went. The driver—and perhaps the intelligent horses—knew the many mud-holes on the six-mile road, especially in the early spring when the frost was coming out of the ground. The worst pulls were over the two steep hills just west of the Dugway. Yet it was a pleasant journey,—at least one judged it must be when Denison students, at the beginning and ending of the school terms, packed the interior of the omnibus and swarmed hilariously over the top of it, carpet bags in hand."

—Ellen Hayes, *Wild Turkeys and Tallow Candles*

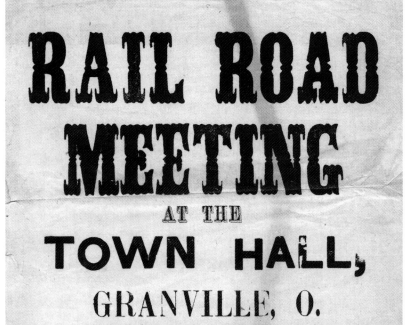

Long without direct railway service, Granville was overjoyed when the Ohio Central came into town on May 29, 1880, and celebrated the event with a grand banquet for the railway hands. The first excursion on construction flatcars ended in tragedy as young William Sinnett was killed after falling between the cars on the return trip. As William T. Utter noted, "Granville's jubilation ended on a tragic note."

(Both images)
Granville Historical Society Archives

RAIL ROAD MEETING AT THE TOWN HALL, GRANVILLE, O.

Saturday Evening, Feb. 21,

Every member of the Soliciting Committee, and every Citizen interested in the Rail Road should be present at this meeting.

Let us all do what our interests demand.

BY ORDER OF THE COMMITTEE.

A flyer for one of many meetings to drum up support for a railroad through Granville.

First Excursion Over the O. C. RAILROAD!

To accommodate those wishing to attend the FESTIVAL AND CONCERT to be given in the Baptist Church at Alexandria, WEDNESDAY EVENING, JUNE 9th, an

EXCURSION TRAIN

Will leave Granville at 7 o'clock, P. M., and returning will leave Alexandria at 9:15 P. M.
The Granville Band will enliven the trip with Music, and the Social at the Church will be made interesting and entertaining by vocal and instrumental music.
Tickets for the round trip, Concert and Festival, can be obtained of G. B. Whiting or A. W. Yale, at 40 cents.

SECURE YOUR TICKETS EARLY.

OHIO CENTRAL RAILROAD,

(BROWN, HOWARD & CO.)

Granville O Station, Jan 5 1881.

Chas.W. Bryant Esq

Dear Sir!

This is to certify that book ticket No 1300 Ohio Central Railroad. was the first ticket sold at this station

Also that ticket No 00 was the first ticket from this Station to Alexandria

Yours truly

C.W Beach

agt. O.C.R.R.

This letter certifies that Number 1300 was the first ticket sold from Granville on the Ohio Central.

The Granville Hat and Shoe Shop took advantage of the railroad's arrival in Granville to issue "tickets" to walk to the store.

(All three images)
Granville Historical Society Archives

Trains puffing through the Raccoon Valley became
a familiar sight, seen here from Sugar Loaf.

(Both images)
Granville Historical Society Archives

Ohio Central Railroad,

TOLEDO DIVISION.

SPECIAL TIME TABLE,

In Effect at 12 o'clock, noon, Sunday, October 10, 1880.

Superceding Special Time Table of October 3d, 1880.

SOUTH AND WEST No. 10. Mixed. A. M.	Total Miles.	STATIONS.	Total Miles from Col.	NORTH AND EAST. No. 11 Mixed. P. M.
6:00	0	Lv......**FOSTORIA**......Ar	140.3	6:45
		8 9		
6:50	8.9	**NEW REIGLE**	131.4	6:00
		2 0		
7:00	10.9	**BERWICK**	129 4	5:50
		3 4		
7:18	14.3	**M'CUTCHENSVILLE**	126 0	5:30
		5.0		
7:43	19.3	**SYCAMORE**	121.0	5:00
		2.6		
7:58	21.9	**PETERSBURG**	118.4	4:45
		3.0		
8:13	24.9	**LEMERT**	115.4	4:30
		8 7		
9:28	33.6	**BUCYRUS**	106.7	3:45
		6.6		
10:05	40.2	**NEW WINCHESTER**	100 1	2:45
		3 4		
10:25	43.6	**THREE LOCUSTS**	96.7	2:25
		7.8		
11:10	51.4	**LEVERING**	88.9	1:45
		1 5		
11:35	52.9	**MT. GILEAD**	87.4	1:35
P. M.		5.0		
12:01	57.9	**LINCOLN CENTER**	82.4	1:05
		5 3		
12:39	63.2	**MARENGO**	77.1	12:39
		4.3		
1 06	67.5	**COUNTY LINE**	72.8	12:19
		4 6		P. M.
1:35	72.1	**CENTERBURG**	68.2	11:59
		4.3		
2:05	76.4	**HARTFORD**	63.9	11:26
		5.9		
2:40	82.3	**JOHNSTOWN**	58.0	10:56
		6 0		
3:05	88.3	**ALEXANDRIA**	52.0	10:16
		5.2		
3:50	93.5	**GRANVILLE**	46.8	9:16
		3 7		
4:02	97.2	**P. H. CROSSING**	43.1	9:00
		5.2		
4:19	102.4	**HEBRON**	37.9	8:40
		3 2		
4:28	105 6	**LAKESIDE**	34.7	8:25
		2.0		
4:35	107.6	**MILLERSPORT**	32.7	8:16
		4.0		
A 4:50	111.6	Ar......**BUSH'S**......Lv.	28.7	D 8:03

Crossing Signals[:

At Pan Handle Crossing.

At Three Locusts for crossing of N. Y. P. & O and Inds. Div, C. C. C. & I. Ry., and at **Berwick Crossing** of the C. S. & C. Flagmen are stationed and will signal train over crossing. No train will be allowed to cross at any of the above points without first receiving signal from Flagman.

Levering.
When Target is placed vertical, O. C. trains will pass. When horizontal, C. C. C. & I. Trains will pass. When diagonal, no train will pass.

Mt. Gilead Short Line.
When Target is placed vertical, O. C. trains will pass. When horizontal, Short Line Trains will pass. When diagonal, no train will pass.

Bucyrus.
A gate at crossing of P. F. W. & C. Ry. has been placed, and no trains will cross until gate keeper has opened the gate.

B. & O. & C. & T. crossing.
When Target is placed horizontal, O. C. trains will pass. When verticle C. & T. trains will pass. When diagonal, B. & O. trains will pass.

Fostoria.
When Target is placed horizontal, O. C. Trains will pass. When diagonal, C. & T. trains will pass. When vertical, L. E. & W. Trains will pass.

W. H. VANDEGRIFT,
Master of Transportation.

G. G. HADLEY,
Gen'l Superintendent.

The Toledo and Ohio Central Granville Depot in 1909. By the 1950s only a few freight cars came into Granville, carrying coal for the Denison heating plant, feed for the mill, or boards for the Granville Lumber Co. All rail service to Granville ceased in 1959.

Granville Historical Society Archives

Horse and buggy with members of the Howe Family on a Granville Street.

Granville Historical Society Archives

Advertisment in *The Granville Times,* Vol. 11 No 7, 10 July, 1890.

The Granville Times

This velocipede, displayed in the Granville Historical Society Museum, was made by Joseph Clouse. He rode it from his home on Clouse Lane to Denison, while he was a student there in the 1860s.

Museum of the Granville Historical Society

Zella Allen Dixson, seen here with her steed "Pegasus," was a familiar sight in Granville. She was Denison's librarian from 1887 to 1890 and spent summers in Granville through the next two decades.

Denison University Archives

"On October 4, 1890, the first car ran from Newark up through beautiful Cherry Valley to Granville. This road furnished a quick and pleasant means of transportation to Granville with the charm of lovely scenery by the way, but it enjoys the additional distinction of having been the longest road of the kind in the world when it was built, and of being the first electric road on record to carry government mail."

—Newark, Ohio, newspaper, ca 1893

Passengers for the Number 9 Interurban car to Newark prepare to board in Granville.

Time Card in Effect Jan. 1, 1903.

Newark & Granville St. Ry. Co.

LV. NEWARK			LV. GRANVILLE	
No. 1	Power House	5:00 am	No. 2	5:30 am
" 3	Squ're	6:00 am	" 4	6:30 am
" 5	B. & O. Depot	7:05 am	" 6	7:45 am
" 7	"	8:30 am	" 8	9:08 am
" 9	"	9:45 am	" 10	10:22 am
" 11	"	11:00 am	" 12	11:37 am
" 13	"	12:15 pm	" 14	12:52 pm
" 15	"	1:30 pm	" 16	2:07 pm
" 17	"	2:45 pm	" 18	3:22 pm
" 19	"	4:00 pm	" 20	4:37 pm
" 21	"	5:15 pm	" 22	5:58 pm
" 23	"	6:35 pm	" 24	7:22 pm
" 25	"	8:00 pm	" 26	8:37 pm
" 27	"	9:20 pm	" 28	9:55 pm
" 29	"	10:45 pm	" 30	11:22 pm

SUNDAY SCHEDULE
LEAVE NEWARK

7:05 am	8:30 am	9:45 am	11:00 am
12:15 pm	1:30 pm	2:45 pm	4:00 pm
5:15 pm	6:35 pm	8:00 pm	9:20 pm

LEAVE GRANVILLE

7:45 am	9:08 am	10:22 am	11:37 am
12:52 pm	2:07 pm	3:22 pm	4:37 pm
5:58 pm	7:22 pm	8:37 pm	9:55 pm

Trains No. 5, 6, 9, 10, 17 and 18 will take Freight. Nos. 5 and 19 connect with the Southbound T. & O. C. Nos. 7 and 23 connect with the Northbound T. & O. C. For Special Car Service, Rates, etc., apply at office, 12 N. Park Place.

TOLEDO & OHIO CENTRAL
TRAINS LEAVE GRANVILLE AS FOLLOWS:

Southbound		Northbound	
" "	7:42 am	" "	9:08 am
	5:22 pm		8:09 pm

T. & O. C. Trains daily except Sunday.

The Interurban Schedule, 1903.

(Both images)
Granville Historical Society Archives

The interurban track, which ran down the middle of Broadway in the center of town *(above)* and beside Mt. Parnassus on East Broadway *(below)*. Granville Historical Society Archives

In July 1916 a lease was executed that allowed the Ohio Electric Railway Company to install tracks for handling freight beside the Old Stone Bank building and make the necessary interior alterations to use it as a depot. This building now houses the museum of the Granville Historical Society.

Granville Historical Society Archives

Denison students board the interurban car in downtown Granville, 1915.

Denison University Archives
Laura Harris Photo Album

Denison students on an omnibus outing, about 1900.

Denison University Archives

People walked; for exercise, to Spring Valley, or out into the country on field trips or picnics. A group of Denison girls sets off, with picnic supplies, about 1915.

Denison University Archives
Laura Harris Photo Album

The Burg Street bridge over Brushy Fork Creek, August 1919. It was one of several covered bridges in the Granville area.

Granville Historical Society Archives

What we now know as the Buxton Inn was built by Orin Granger in 1812. It was a stop on the stage route between Zanesville and Worthington. It has been operated as an inn since its construction. This view shows the inn as it appeared in the 1860s when it was known as the Dilley House. In 1971, Orville and Audrey Orr purchased it from Nell Schoeller and restored it to its original 19th-century color and appearance.

Granville Historical Society Archives

The Mansion House, built in 1820 on the corner of Broadway and Prospect Streets, rivaled the Buxton in popularity. The mob that had incited the 1836 anti-abolitionist riot gathered there. Its last proprietor refused to stop serving liquor and for his failure to do so was dropped from the rolls of the Presbyterian Church.

Granville Historical Society Archives

In 1924, J. S. Jones opened the Granville Inn, built on the site of the Granville Female College (1827–1898). The gymnasium, at the rear of the lot, was saved when the college building was demolished in 1908; it became the Inn's garage. When the Kent Group purchased and refurbished the Inn in 1976, this building was incorporated into the Inn as additional guest rooms. The Inn accommodated important guests to Denison University and Granville and has been the setting for many weddings, celebrations, and organization meetings. The inn has recently changed ownership and undergone major renovations.

(Both images)
Granville Historical Society Archives

The Mansion House was demolished in 1886 to make way for the Hotel Granville beside the 1862 G. T. Jones Building. The hotel could accommodate 100 guests. These three-storey brick buildings housed many businesses over the years. Geach Hardware, Piper Meat Market, and the Perry Grocery store are shown in this photo from the 1890s. The small building at the right in the photograph housed Granville's telephone exchange. Remembered by many as Gregory Hardware, these buildings were demolished in 1967 to make way for a Marathon Gasoline station. In 2001, the gasoline station made way for the relocated Taylor Drug Store. (See pages 68 and 69.)

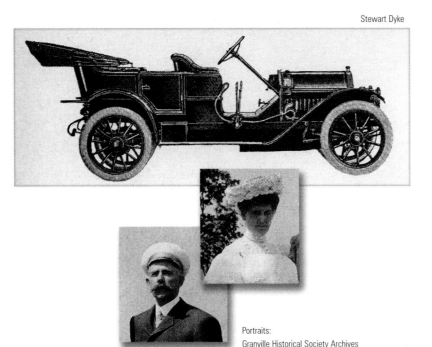

Stewart Dyke

Portraits:
Granville Historical Society Archives

As the railroad and interurban replaced travel by canal, gasoline-powered vehicles slowly preempted railway travel. By 1912, more than a dozen Granville families owned automobiles. Burton and Dora Case made a trip in a Hudson Touring Car *(see example, top)* from Granville to Long Island, New York, in June 1912.

Mrs. Case wrote an account of their journey for *The Granville Times*, entitled "About Good Roads."

The following are excerpts from Mrs. Case's article:

"On the morning of June 28 at a quarter past seven, the new 1912 'Hudson 33' driven by the owner, accompanied by his wife, started on its 900 mile journey, via Delaware, Bucyrus, Elyria, Cleveland, Buffalo, etc., to New York . . . made Cleveland that evening with the speedometer registering 200 miles and Westfield the next afternoon at 2:30 o'clock speedometer at 340 miles. These distances were materially increased on account of the frequent detours demanded by the almost universal road building or repairing throughout the whole country. . . . One of the discomforts attendant on motoring through this state is the absence of sign posts of any sort. To be sure the *Columbus Dispatch* has 'blazed the trail' in several directions from the capital city, but there remains a great work to be done by Ohio Automobile Clubs in erecting danger signals, as well as 'pointing fingers' for the convenience of tourists."

She comments on the superiority of New York Roads over those in Ohio:

"From Albany to Poughkeepsie one drives over roads as hard and smooth as a floor and his machine takes the stiff grades at high speed as easily as it takes the level stretches. When we consider that the automobile has come to stay and that it soon will be the only vehicle used not only for pleasure but also for trucking, we can appreciate the value of good roads to a community as well as to a commonwealth. . . . Long Island is a motorists paradise, every road in fine condition, every one leading to some interesting resort. There is no dust, no dirt, no coal smoke, even a smoking auto being barred from the parks. The principal thoroughfares are lighted by electricity at night, so that the auto head lights are unnecessary."

She admonishes Granville to improve:

"Granville never looked more attractive than when we returned from this outing. She possesses so many natural advantages that it seems a pity she should be deprived of the most obvious ones of all, fine streets and an adequate sewer system. A smooth well oiled automobile road through the center of Broadway with side tracks for horses would add greatly to the attractiveness of the village in the eyes of strangers and increase the pleasure of its inhabitants, by making the drive through its streets less of a penance than is now the case."

—*The Granville Times* 8 August, 1912, p. 1

Regular bus service to Granville began in the early 1920s. The bus was owned by Carl Wyant.

(Both images)
Granville Historical Society Archives

Dora Case, at right, and Clara Sinnett White ride past in a touring car, ca 1925.

Denison student volunteers load a new model Studebaker for a "Hill Climb" test on Thresher Street about 1930. Professor Richard Howe, fifth from the left, supervises the effort.

An automobile crosses the Lancaster Road Bridge over Raccoon Creek in 1914.

(Above and left)
Granville Historical Society Archives

West Broadway, May 1950. The transition to automobiles was complete on Granville's streets. Horseback riding had become an equestrian sport.

Sidney Hollingworth, courtesy of Florence Hollingworth Wright

"The engineers at the State Highway Office, Newark, tell the *Booster* that eight of a total of seventy parcels of right of way have now been acquired, and the remainder will be cleared up as rapidly as possible this fall. Contracts can be let approximately six weeks after all the right of way has been settled. Such preliminary work as is possible is now being done by a Columbus engineering firm. Settling a rumor that the by-pass would not permit access from Cherry Valley Road, the engineers stated this week that access will be possible at a grade level crossing."

—*The Granville Booster*, August 25, 1960

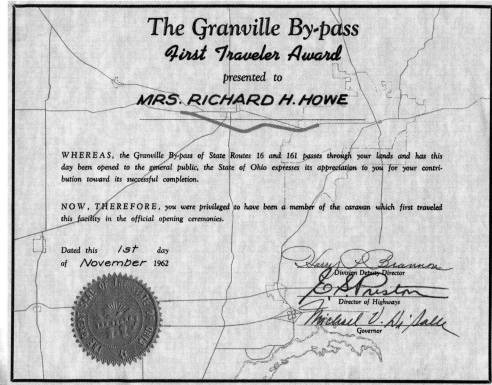

The Granville By-pass
First Traveler Award
presented to
MRS. RICHARD H. HOWE

WHEREAS, the Granville By-pass of State Routes 16 and 161 passes through your lands and has this day been opened to the general public, the State of Ohio expresses its appreciation to you for your contribution toward its successful completion.

NOW, THEREFORE, you were privileged to have been a member of the caravan which first traveled this facility in the official opening ceremonies.

Dated this 1st day of November 1962

Division Deputy Director
Director of Highways
Governor

Granville Historical Society Archives

Large trucks are a familiar sight today in Granville on Ohio State Route 661, Main Street, Broadway, and Pearl Street.

The Granville Sentinel

Pausing to chat on Broadway, 1979.

CHAPTER 10

Living in Granville

"A good town to live in" seems to be the theme of much that has been written and spoken about Granville. The stimulation of the presence of Denison University coupled with a well-educated population has assured a lively life style for its citizens. At the beginning of the 21st century the downtown is the scene, as it always has been, of almost constant activity. Sidewalks are bustling from dawn to dark with walkers and bikers, and annual special events draw crowds. Throughout the village and township opportunities for recreation, passive and active, abound. Most of all, however, Granville citizens enjoy their homes, historic and otherwise, and treasure their families.

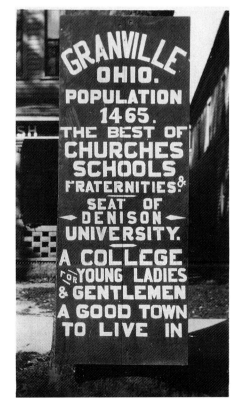

This sign stood in front of 226 East Broadway, then a grocery store, in the 1920s.

Granville Historical Society Archives

189

The Welsh settlers of 1802 were the first permanent landowners who left a written record of their lives. This map locates sites important to their history.

(Both images)
Granville Historical Society Archives

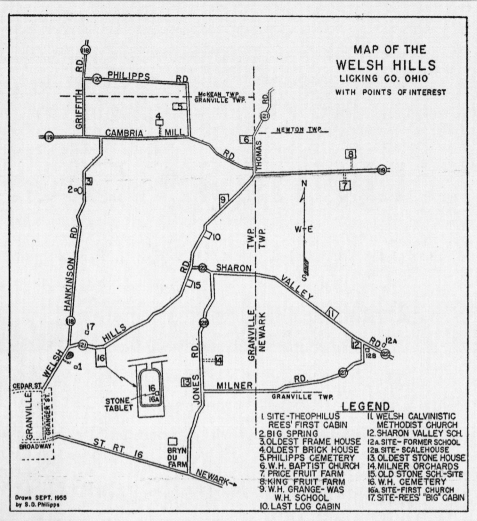

MAP OF THE
WELSH HILLS
LICKING CO. OHIO
WITH POINTS OF INTEREST

LEGEND
1. SITE-THEOPHILUS REES' FIRST CABIN
2. BIG SPRING
3. OLDEST FRAME HOUSE
4. OLDEST BRICK HOUSE
5. PHILIPPS CEMETERY
6. W.H. BAPTIST CHURCH
7. PRICE FRUIT FARM
8. KING FRUIT FARM
9. W.H. GRANGE- WAS W.H. SCHOOL
10. LAST LOG CABIN
11. WELSH CALVINISTIC METHODIST CHURCH
12. SHARON VALLEY SCH.
12a. SITE- FORMER SCHOOL
12b. SITE- SCALEHOUSE
13. OLDEST STONE HOUSE
14. MILNER ORCHARDS
15. OLD STONE SCH.-SITE
16. W.H. CEMETERY
16a. SITE-FIRST CHURCH
17. SITE-REES "BIG" CABIN

Drawn SEPT. 1955 by S.D. Philipps

This cabin was old when it was photographed some time before 1900. It is said to have been the home of Theophilus Rees, the leader of the first Welsh families in the township. His grandson, T. J. Thomas, is seated on the porch, holding a Welsh-language bible.

A gathering of Welsh families, about 1870 or a little earlier. Some of the family names represented include Thomas, Glynn, Evans, and Philipps.

The Thomas Cramer home on Hankinson Road in 1905. Grace Owens leads little Wilbur Hankinson into the drive.

The Hankinson family pose in front of their home. Note the lawn mower at rest at the left.

Living in Granville includes enjoying leisure time. In the next few pages we have pictured some of the varied ways Granvillians have amused and entertained themselves and others.

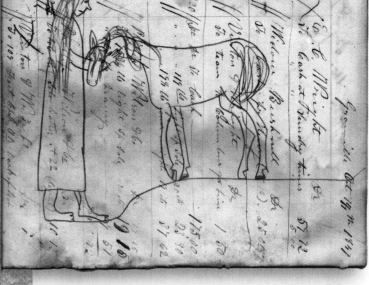

In earlier times, a child with the urge to create couldn't just run down to the store and buy crayons and coloring paper. One artistic youngster was given an old ledger, dated 1847, to use.

(All images on this page and facing page)
Granville Historical Society Archives

Political fervor gripped Ohio during the 1888 presidential elections. Throughout the state, the log-cabin campaign of William Henry Harrison was invoked by supporters of his grandson, Republican Benjamin Harrison. During the 1840 campaign, a log cabin had been built and paraded to Newark with much celebration. In 1888, an unsuccessful effort was made to find that cabin, so a new one, pictured here, was built. A club of men who had voted for the original Harrison was formed, some of whom pose in front of the structure.

Card games made a long afternoon or evening go quickly. This foursome is playing at *The Granville Times* print shop and includes Lou Kussmaul, Ike DeBow, "Howdy" Howe, and Billy McDonald. A note on the photo says that the electric light was powered by the interurban trolley via Ackley's drug store.

Baseball was the national pastime around 1900. The area of Weaver Drive and Lancaster Road was the location of this diamond.

Strolling was a popular activity on a fine day. These ladies, Anna Howe Jones, Blanche Horton, and Mamie Jones, rest on a visit to Maple Grove Cemetery, dressed in their Sunday best.

There stands the "Sugar-Loaf", bare, bald and bold; For years her top has smoked and fires uprolled. Cremating Livy or the Calculus.
— J. W. Weddell. —

In 1896 a citizens' group decided to act on making the hill a park, an idea that had been discussed for several years. An announcement was made for a "civic carnival" to implement reforestation. The day-long event resulted in over 300 saplings being brought in and planted, often in memory of loved-ones. This photo, taken a few years later from Barney Science Building, shows the results of the effort.

Only 85 years after settlement, the hill called "stone hill" or Sugar Loaf was barren. The trees had been felled for lumber and firewood, and one side was quarried. In addition, citizens found the area a free source of fill dirt and rubble for the many damp areas in town. When this photo was published, students at Denison University held annual ceremonies at the top, where they burned their textbooks upon completion of their courses. From *Granville, a Pleasant Memory*, by Thalia Amelia Ralston and William G. Tight, 1899.

(All images on this page)
Granville Historical Society Archives

Wilson's or Collins' Spring was just west of and across Broadway from Sugar Loaf.

The Thomas J. Evans bike path connecting Newark and Johnstown by way of Granville is a popular recreational area in all seasons.

The Granville Recreation Commission sponsored this girls basketball team about 1988.

The Robert Drake Family

(Below)
The Granville Sentinel

Tennis lessons for this young group were held at the tennis club near Spring Valley Pool on Columbus Road, about 1990. Leisha Hurwitz photograph.

Boys and girls enjoy playing soccer. Here a group of boys is learning some of the basics.

(Above and top left)
The Granville Sentinel

Lake Hudson was a former gravel pit developed into a swimming and boating area by the Williams family.

The Granville Sentinel

Young men on a hot summer day, about 1920. Swimming holes like this one could be unsafe, and were certainly not normally available for young ladies.

Granville Historical Society Archives

Spring Valley Pool, owned by the Roberts family, was a favorite summer spot for many decades. Here swimmers cool off in 1953. In 2004 its future was uncertain.

Roberts Family, courtesy of Anne Ormond

Two of the Colwell daughters with the family Christmas tree in the 1890s.

(Above right and left)
Granville Historical Society Archives

Winter brings a different type of fun. The Colwell children grew up in a large house on College Hill. They seem to have used up almost all the nearby snow in making this creature, about 1897.

"There were three large ponds pretty close to town [in about 1816] and the chief sport of all the children in winter was sliding down the hill south of our house and sliding on these ponds."—Chloe L. Harris, born in Granville in 1810. Children in 2004 still love to sled on Granville's hills.

(Bottom left and right)
The Granville Sentinel

A quiet walk on a Broadway sidewalk decked out for the holidays.

Through the years, Broadway downtown was the place to go, to see, and to be seen. These gentlemen were continuing a tradition of people-watching from the street side benches. George Grogan is second from the left, and Jerry Ackley is on the right. They are in front of the building on the southwest corner of Prospect and Broadway, which later housed the village offices and police station.

Granville Historical Society Archives

Young men and cars seem to belong together. Showing off a 1941 automobile sold to Lloyd Philipps are Donald Josif, Ed Pinkerton, Tom Ramsay, and Bernie Williams.

The Williams Family

In 1975 Taylor's Drug Store was about the last place in town to close for the night, at 9 pm. A group could usually be found outside on fine nights.

Anestis Diakopoulos, used with permission

The shops on Broadway have come and gone, and their focus has changed from necessities to niceties. Lynne Windley discusses her wares with Randy French and his daughter Abbie in about 1995. The shop was at 226 East Broadway.

(Above and bottom two images)
The Granville Sentinel

The population of Granville likes to read. An addition to the library was dedicated in 1970, which necessitated a new entrance on the east side. The alley, which had been a convenient place to drop off children and books, was later made into a no-traffic court for pedestrian safety.

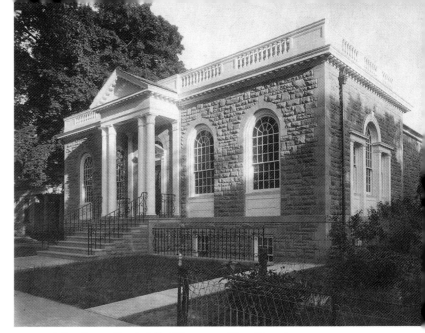

The Granville Public Library on East Broadway as it appeared when newly constructed in 1925.

Granville Historical Society Archives

Esther Coffey was known to most residents in the 1970s-1990s. She sometimes could be found gathering aluminum cans by the bagful, which she sold for recycling. She used the profits to buy flowers to plant around the town. Esther was a member of the Town and Country Garden Club, and is seen here at one of their sidewalk plant sales.

East Broadway has been the site of many restaurants catering to families. One of the most enduring has been The Aladdin, "Home of the Fudge Cake." Long-time chef Don Snelling looks over some breakfast items.

Family picnics were a good source of fun, especially during the Great Depression, when cash for entertainment was scarce. Here are members of the Young, Howe, and Hall families on a Sunday outing.

Granville Historical Society Archives

One restaurant that was not on Broadway was The Evergreens, which opened in about 1951 at 1771 Columbus Road, just past Spring Valley. The simple family atmosphere made it a good place for a quick meal. It was especially popular with employees of the nearby Owens Corning Fiberglas technical center. A fire in 2001 caused it to be closed and razed.

By the end of the twentieth century, the sidewalks of East Broadway were filled in summer by outdoor dining areas. One of the first to set up umbrellas and tables was Victoria's Parlour at 134. Gayle Jackson is seen here serving Fred Palmer.

(Left and top two images)
The Granville Sentinel

Social organizations have been beloved by Granville citizens for many years. One of the longest-lived was the Fortnightly Club, which became the Fortnightly Travelers Club after a merger. Here members recreate a colonial moment in 1899.

(Above and below)
Granville Historical Society Archives

Costume parties are enjoyed by young and old. These children were attending a Halloween party at the Fuson home on Shepardson Court, about 1990. Their families were members of the New Friends Food Co-op, so the costume theme was fruits or vegetables. Back row: Laurel Fuson, Shamsi Tower, Christopher Poppa, Anyi Onyido. Front: Ifeanyi Onyido, Tyler Southard, and Hannah Fuson. Leisha Hurwitz photograph.

The Granville Sentinel

A costume party and nothing to wear? These quick-thinking parents borrowed uniforms from the Marching Blue Aces and went as Alexander's Ragtime Band.

The Robert Drake Family

During the national bicentennial of 1976 all things historical were celebrated. Bill Holloway, dressed as Simon Kenton, displays his home-made percussion rifle.

Granville Historical Society Archives

Granville Daughters of the American Revolution entertain in the early 1950s. From the left, Mrs. Fred Detweiler; Priscilla Stark, Denison University Dean of Women; Goldie Howe; Mary Fitch; and Madelyn Rupp.

Music is a welcome ingredient of a day or evening in Granville. Bob Kunkle, Oscar Ball, Troy Herdman, and Gaylord Johnson play in front of Taylor's at its 132 East Broadway location.

The Welsh Hills Band entertained at the Masonic picnic at Cat Run. Back row: E. Wright, Archie Hankinson, S. Jones, C. Hartman, J. Hankinson, H. Griffith, W. Parry, H. Williams, leader. Front row: F. Hartman, T. Parry, B. Williams, G. Griffith, Albert Hankinson, P. Philipps, C. Thompson.

Denison University students and their friends often got up elaborate entertainments to which the whole town was invited. One recurring event was the "singin' skewl," a parody of the more staid recitals which were frequently presented by the various music classes.

(Right and top right)
Granville Historical
Society Archives

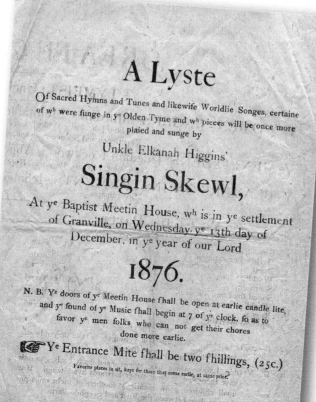

A Lyste

Of Sacred Hymns and Tunes and likewife Worldlie Songes, certaine of wᵇ were funge in yᵉ Olden Tyme and wᵇ pieces will be once more plaied and funge by

Unkle Elkanah Higgins'

Singin Skewl,

At yᵉ Baptist Meetin House, wᵇ is in yᵉ settlement of Granville, on Wednesday, yᵉ 13th day of December, in yᵉ year of our Lord

1876.

N. B. Yᵉ doors of yᵉ Meetin House fhall be open at earlie candle lite, and yᵉ found of yᵉ Music fhall begin at 7 of yᵉ clock, fo as to favor yᵉ men folks who can not get their chores done more earlie.

☞ Yᵉ Entrance Mite fhall be two fhillings, (25c.)

Favorite places to sit, kept for those that come earlie, at same price.

Photo; Charles Peterson

The Granville Recreation Commission began to sponsor its Concerts on the Green in 1982, bringing musical groups to town from far and near. The Dutton Family was a favorite, returning for several years. Here Abigail Dutton plays to the audience in 1996.

(Above and top left)
The Granville Sentinel

Weddings are big events for some families, presenting good occasions for entertaining relatives and old friends. This more intimate meal was attended by at least one Granville fellow, Frank Robinson, who is seated with his back to the camera. The family is not identified.

Granville Life-Style Museum

Many sons and daughters of Granville choose to be married "at home." Weddings large and small have been a highlight of life in Granville.

"Bethia Linnel at the age of 19 was married to Rev. Timothy Harris [on] September 4, 1809 thus becoming the wife of the Pastor of the first church in Granville. It is said the wedding of Rev. and Mrs. Harris was a social event of great importance in which the surrounding county were bidden to participate, as social caste was unknown at that time. The cabin being small the ceremony was performed out of doors, the guests being seated on trees felled for that purpose. The bride's dress was of changeable silk and made by the one dressmaker living in Newark. The wedding journey to Marietta was made on horseback."

Excerpt from the Linnel family records in the Granville Historical Society archives .

Photo: Don Pound Studio, used with permission

On July 20, 1996, this wedding party paused in front of Taylor's Drug Store. The bride, the groom, and most of the wedding party were graduates of Granville High School. Front row: Stephanie Dicus, Lori Thompson ('88), Amy Boldon ('88). Regina Ormond, bride Kristine Treece ('88), Brett Wilhelm ('85), Brian Gutreuter, Ben Johnson, Matt Treece ('94), Jeff Hinebaugh ('85). Back row: Greg Treece ('91), Brant Clark ('85), Nate Card ('85), groom Guy Michael ('85), Jeff Michael ('88), Sara Wiper Sharp ('85), Kim Snively Stryker, Nicki Jiran ('88), Holly James Michael, Debbie Schnaidt Johnson ('85), Brian Rapp ('78) and Nancy Cope.

Treece Family

The wedding of Jere Ackley and Anna Cozad took place in St. Luke's Episcopal Church in the 1940s.

(Both images)
Granville Historical Society Archives

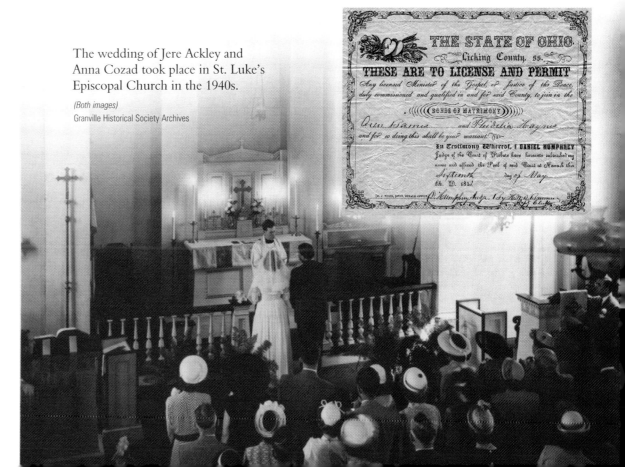

A family portrait at the home at 2455 Old Columbus Road as it looked in 1894. Front row: Hayesel Huston (Eaton), age 5, Libbie Wilkin Carter, Enos Wilkin, Wilkin Jones, Nancy Holmes Wilkin, James Huston, Jr., Amanda Wilkin Huston, Nanette Huston (Bartlett), age 6. Back: H. Judson Carter, Sophronia Carter, Calla Wilkin Jones, Timothy B. Jones, James A. Huston.

George Wales

Life in Granville focuses on families. One of the families which came with the first settlers from New England and still has a presence here in 2004 is Everett. This large tintype, taken in the 1860s, is labeled simply "some of the older Everetts."

The Roberts family poses outside their home at 214 South Cherry about 1915.

Roberts Family, courtesy of Anne Ormond

The interior of the home at 5230 Worthington Road, sometimes referred to as Moots Run Farm. Notice the family photographs decorating the mantle.

One of the bedrooms of the Sinnett Mt. Parnassus home.

One of the first citizens of Granville to move to "the suburbs" was Dr. Edwin Sinnett, when he built his fine house on Mt. Parnassus. He sits here in his doorway with horse and buggy at the ready.

This is a picture of the home at Bryn Du when it belonged to the McCune family and was called Fort Hill, for the Native American earthworks behind it on the hill. This house was eventually surrounded by and enclosed within the walls of the present much larger structure, which was sold to the Village of Granville in 2004 .

On the porch at Mt. Parnassus, playing with the Sinnett family dog.

The brick home built by Gerard Bancroft in 1824 at 120 East Elm has been remodeled, and is now bordered by the driveway of a bank on each side. Bancroft was a popular house builder and carpenter in the village. His large shop filled the lot behind the house.

Every time a home changes owners, the home itself is changed, often beyond recognition. The following photos might provoke a reaction of "I know that house, but where is it?" or "so that's what it looked like!" Warner and Carrie Little Devinney (also spelled Devenney) moved several times during their married lives. Here they sit on the front porch of their home on the far east end of Elm Street.

Denison University librarian Zella Allen Dixson in her parlor at 324 West Elm Street, about 1890.

Denison University Archives

These homes sit on Elm Street at each side of the alley leading to the library. At the time of this picture the Raymond family owned the one on the left, built by Ashley Bancroft in 1825. The little house on the right is known as the "clockmaker's house" after the occupation of its first owner, Charles French.

(Above and top two images)
Granville Historical Society Archives

A lovely home on North Plum, its porch festooned with vines.

Granville Historical Society Archives

When the Richards family moved in 1947, Granville was a small village, and this house, at the intersection of North and New Burg Streets, was considered to be out of town.

The William T. Richards Family, courtesy of Patricia Battiston

Ken and Carol Apacki and their daughters Mary Kay, Erin, and Leslie, in front of their home at 410 West Maple. In 1975 the Apacki family and Granville were photographed for an article in a Russian language magazine on life in an American small town.

Anestis Diakopoulos, used with permission

William T. Utter, PhD, professor of history at Denison University, dictates a page of his book *Granville, the Story of an Ohio Village* (1956).

CHAPTER 11

Recording It All

The recording of Granville's history was begun by the secretary of the Licking Land Company in 1804. He carefully detailed the deliberations and contributions of company members when they planned for the purchase of their new homeland. But beyond the taking of minutes, someone had to keep the documents. And someone else had to care for them, keeping them clean and protected from the elements and vermin. And still someone else had to read and reread them, then transcribe the faded handwriting into type so that they could be read as easily as a page in a book. Our knowledge of the first settlers' activities depends on all these "someones," and many more. This chapter details the importance of the savers and the story-tellers, the reporters and the rescuers, the preservers and picture-makers and presenters.

Howard Malcolm Sedgwick spent several years photographing Granville people and scenes in the 1870s. He later moved to Zanesville where he died in 1892 at the age of 49.

THE WANDERER.

PUBLISHED AT GRANVILLE, LICKING COUNTY, OHIO, BY SERENO WRIGHT.

FRIDAY, MARCH. 14, 1823.

Sereno Wright, 1779-1858, arrived in Granville in 1814 from Vermont. He was an early school teacher and postmaster, and at his home at the lot now numbered 121 South Main Street he ran a small merchandise store. It was at this place in 1822 and 1823 that he published Granville's first newspaper, *The Wanderer*. Sereno was active in public service, holding the office of County Treasurer from 1827 to 1837.

The Intelligencer was published from 1848 until 1851. Like many newspapers of its time, it focused on national and political news. Its greatest value for historians lies in its advertisements, which were local, and in some of its editorial content.

All four images:

Granville Historical Society Archives

Granville Intelligencer.

VOL. 1.   GRANVILLE; WEDNESDAY, SEPTEMBER 6, 1848.   NO. 1.

Painstaking attention to detail is the hallmark of both the images on this page, although the sources and subjects could hardly have less in common.

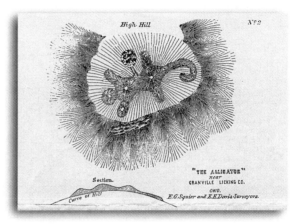

In the 1840s E. G. Squier and E. H. Davis carefully mapped Native American earthworks throughout Ohio, publishing them in 1848 as part of *Ancient Monuments of the Mississippi Valley*. Here is their plan of Granville's most famous hilltop.

Squier and Davis, *Ancient Monuments of the Mississippi Valley*

The Reverend Jacob Little was the long-time pastor of the Congregational Church in the Village. His meticulously kept records of deaths in the area were part of his annual New Year's Day sermons. His recordings took place during a period when there were no newspapers in Granville, so are invaluable as resources for genealogists.

Granville Historical Society Archives

Mortality of Granville Township in 1855, from Mr. Little's Annual Sermon.

DATE.	NAME.	DISEASE.	AGE.
January 1,	Lewis, son of Rowland Hughes,	Typhus Fever,	15 y.
" 13,	Mrs Hannah Garno,	Typhoid Fever,	29 y.
" 20,	Alma L., daughter of John Sinnet,	"	5 y.
" 24,	Cary Albert, son of Albert Jones,	Cause unknown,	2 m.
" 23,	Miss Clara Pettibone,	Consumption,	25 y.
" 30,	Infant son of L. S. Twining,	Hooping Cough,	20 d.
February 3,	Charles Barnes. son of J. H. Bancroft,	"	33 m.
" 8,	Abraham Walker,	Consumption,	44 y.
" 13,	Abigail R., wife of H. B. Camp,	"	25 y.
" 27,	Lydia, widow of Oliver Dickinson,	Old Age,	87 y.
March 6,	Jeremiah W. Ackley,	Consumption,	28 y.
" 7,	Samuel Remington,	Old Age,	84 y.
" 16,	Rebecca, wife of Thomas Cramer,	Cancered Stomach,	72 y.
April 1,	Jeremiah French,	Consumption,	68 y.
" 10,	Orlena, daughter of Horace Wolcott,	"	20 y.
" 12,	Samuel Elmer, son of John Wood,	Croup,	2 y.
May 4,	Elizabeth, widow of David Thomas,	Dyspepsia,	73 y.
" 14,	Harriet M., daghter of Seymour Wood,	Congestive Fever,	27 y.
" 16,	Infant son of H. C Paige,	Fits,	3 d.
" 24,	Jewett, son of S. G. Everitt,	Inflamed Brain,	6 m.
" "	Adah, widow of Justin Hillyer,	Old Age,	79 y.
June 11,	Arthur Andrews. son of S. N. Sanford,	Dysentery,	1 y.
" 14,	Stephen Brown, at the Infirmary,	Old Age,	69 y.
July 7,	Otis Winter, son of Hall Robertson,	Typhoid Fever,	8 y.
" 21,	Wm. Wallace, son of Wm Johnson,	Dysentery,	23 m.
" "	Matilda, daughter of Thomas Ephland,	Consumption,	5 w.
" 23	Geo Washington, son of Sheldon Swan,	Dysentery,	12 y.
August 1,	Martha Helen, daughter of Sheldon Swan	"	17 y.
" 4,	Infant daughter of T. N Weeks,	Cholera Infantum,	29 d.
" 5,	Infant daughter of T. N. Weeks,	"	30 d.
" 7,	Rachel, wife of Elias Gilman,	Dysentery,	80 y.
" "	Frederick W., son of John Gardner,	Congestion of the Brain,	18 m.
" 13	Hugh Dennis,	Dysentery,	45 y.
" 14	Rosaltha Orlinda, daughter of Thos. Wells,	"	12 y.
" "	John Bradley, son of Bradley Camp.	"	5 y.
" 19,	Mary Ann, wife of Rev. B. Lowe,	"	50 y.
" 21,	Clinton Sage, son of L. A. Roberts,	Diarrhoea,	16 m.
" 29,	Daniel Davies,	Urinal detention,	64 y.
Sept'er 7,	Infant daughter of John Minton,	Dysentery	2 w.
" 10,	Hervey Ingham, son of J. D. Jones,	Ulceration of Bowels,	3 y.
" 12,	Eugene Nichols, at Infirmary,	Dysentery,	20 y.
" 13,	William P. Harper,	"	72 y.
" "	Nancy Amelia, daughter of J R. Clark,	Remittent Fever,	4 y.
" 15,	Lyman Howard, son of J. R. Clark,	"	5 y.
" 16,	Simeon Reed,	Congestive Fever,	62 y.
" 20,	Lucy Lavisa. wife of John Minton,	Dysentery,	38 y.
" 22,	Emeline Subra, daughter of Milo Rose,	Congestive Fever,	14 y.
" "	Miss Marie Wilson, at the Infirmary,	Dysentery,	24 y.
" 28,	Dea. Eli Butler,	Ulcerated Stomach,	63 y.
October 2	John Westley Hobart,	Consumption,	26 y.
" 6	Timothy A. Smith,	"	41 y.
" 7,	Martha Amelia, dau. of Hervey Nichols,	"	16 y.
" 13	Content, widow of Samuel Remington,	Bilious Fever,	78 y.
" 15,	Lewis Jones, son of B B. Loar,	Dropsy,	20 m.
" 16,	Julia, daughter of Van Browning,	Brain Fever,	13 y.
" 22,	Cudjoe Wyche, manumitted slave,	Old Age,	86 y.
" 23	Mary, wife of James Shorter,	Consumption,	19 y.
Nov'r 20,	Lucy Melissa, wife of David Partridge,	Dysentery,	26 y.
" 27,	Hannah, wife of Ralph Granger,	Heart Disease.	59 y.
" "	Martha, wife of Edward Nicol,	Clothes taking fire,	76 y.
Dec'r 20,	Hiram Rose,	Old Age,	89 y.
" 23,	Jemima, wife of Ashley Graves,	Diseased Stomach,	53 y.
" 27,	John A. Gardner,	Typhoid Pneumonia,	33 y.

In January, died 6; February, 4; March, 3; April, 3; May, 5; June, 2; July, 4; August, 11; September, 11; October. 8; November. 3; December, 3;—adults, 39—children, 24;—total, 63—more than twice the average of the ten preceding years. The sickness of the West in 1855, is attributed to plowing an unusual quantity, the constant rain, or the abundant vegetation. By six years comparing our township with four others, 40 miles from the sea. in New England, it has been proved that our mortality is nearly seven per cent. less than theirs. Our place never having the cholera, is a city of refuge when the scourge prevails. In 1855, we lost by dysentery, 15; consumption, 11; and old age, 6. Five of the deceased were past 80 years of age, and there are still living eighteen past 80, and seventy-five past 70, in our population of 2300.

Not long before the invention of photography in 1839, this was the style of quickly-drawn portraiture commonly available. Marcus Root, born in Granville Township in 1808, was the artist who drew Charlotte Spelman. The original drawing is in the Avery-Downer House museum, once the home of Charlotte's sister.

(All four images)
Granville Historical Society Archives

The next step in photography was the ambrotype, in which a weak negative image on glass was backed with dark material making it visible as a positive image. Both daguerreotypes and ambrotypes were protected by cases of leather or other hard materials. These images were widely popular because they were portable but extremely clear and true to life.

TO DAGUERREOTYPISTS.

ON hand, and for sale, a complete assortment of Cameras—one quarter and half plate size of the real Voightlander & Son's and American make, Coating boxes, Buffing irons, Gilding stands, Prepared buckskins, and cotton. Also Plates, Cases, Chemicals, and a fine assortment of Lockets and Breastpins, designed expressly for Daguerreotype Miniatures.—Arrangements have been made at M. A. Root's celebrated establishment in Philadelphia, for a constant supply of the above and all other articles used by the Profession.   A. P. PRICHARD.
Granville, Sept. 6, 1848.

Marcus Root set up a studio for a few months in Granville, above Anthony Prichard's drug store. Afterward, he continued to provide all the necessary supplies for local photographers.

Marcus Root left Granville in 1830 for the East Coast. He studied drawing and developed a system of penmanship. A few years later the first form of photography, the daguerreotype, was developed. Marcus learned the new art, becoming one of its more famous practitioners in Philadelphia and New York. He wrote what some considered the first book on photography, *The Camera and the Pencil*, in 1864. Marcus died in Philadelphia in 1888.

Frank Carter, 1831-1894, was a prolific photographer at about the time of the Civil War. A collection of over 1500 glass negatives from his studio, only part of his output, is in the archives of the Granville Historical Society. Although most of the subjects' names are not known, their portraits are honest representations, with untouched wrinkles, freckles, and rumpled clothing.

(All four images)
Granville Historical Society Archives

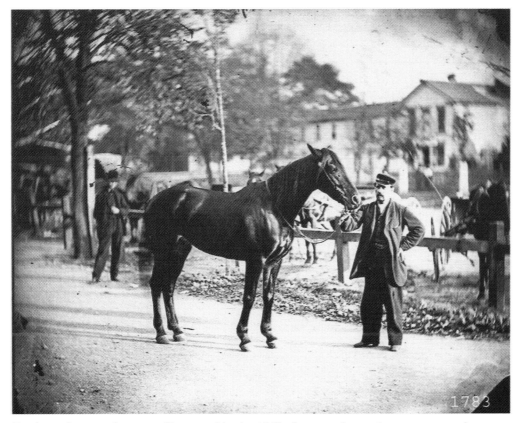

Outdoor photography was still unusual in the 1860s, because the equipment was cumbersome and the proper conditions could be better controlled in the studio. This horse paused for its portrait by Carter on Broadway approximately at the mid-block crosswalk's north end.

In 2002 Duane Dawley of Newark, Ohio, began the labor of scanning each of Carter's three by four inch glass negatives and generating eight by ten inch prints. The uncropped prints give fascinating glimpses of Carter's studio and accouterments. Notice the head clamp behind the mother's left side. Normally this would have been used to keep the subject's head still and the picture unblurred during the long exposure time necessary. Here the mother, who is busy keeping Baby still, would probably have been cropped out.

Samuel Porter Tresize, 1839-1925, was active intermittently in Granville for many years, taking portraits, group photographs, and scenes. He was the official photographer of the village centennial in 1905.

S. P. Tresize was a practitioner of the art of stereographic photography, using a special camera which took two slightly different images. The stereograph was looked at by means of a special viewer, and produced a somewhat three-dimensional picture. This view is of the Edwin Sinnett home on East Broadway, on the site of the library.

A good example of a Tresize family portrait. Here Denison Professor W.G. Tight poses with his wife Arabella and two children, Dexter and Minnie.

A source of many bits of information about Granville in the 1860s-1890s was the Denison University publication, *The Collegian.* Editorial commentary often included observations of activities in and around town, and advertisements like those shown gave glimpses of everyday life.

S. P. Tresize. Granville, Ohio.

945 O St. N. W.

Washington, D. C. May 4/80

Dear Friend,

I was very much gratified and interested in reading your good letter of Ap. 30. It will give me the greatest pleasure to aid you all I can in your good work & I have no doubt you and Mr Bryant will make achieve great success. I write now chiefly to say that I will send your pictures by the first mail to Brother Henry, with my remarks, & your letter. I made out the pictures they first thing before I read your letter. So you see your sketches must be very good. My impression is that the steeple of the Pres. church (in my boyish days every body called it meeting house) was rather straighter than you represent it, & taller, and the ball fitted closer on top of the steeple — being the base and

As the 75th anniversary of the founding of Granville Village approached, The Reverend Henry Bushnell and Charles Webster Bryant conceived the idea of writing a history. Bushnell took up the recording of the action, while Bryant concentrated on genealogies. Both men engaged in voluminous correspondence with former residents, asking questions about early memories and "who married whom?" In the letter reproduced here, William Richards writes to Bushnell commenting on some drawings of early buildings which Bushnell had sent for confirmation. The drawings and memories became part of *The History of Granville, Licking County, Ohio*, published in 1889.

Charles Webster Bryant, 1849-1886, founder of the Granville Historical Society. His genealogical work on the first settlers of the town was interrupted by his early death at age 37.

[734] In memory of William Son of Charles & Mary Root died July 22 1824 aged 13 Mo. 16 days.

Happy infant early blest Rest in peaceful slumber rest

[The above on a small freestone slab standing about 6 ft. S. of the central roadway]

[735] In memory of Elizabeth daughter of Charles & Mary Root died Dec 7 1825 aged 5 years & 2 days

So fades the lovely blooming flower Frail smiling solace of an hour So all our earthly comforts fly And pleasures only bloom to die

[The above on a freestone slab that has fallen E.]

[736] William Son of Charles and Mary Root died Dec.n the 30 1827 Aged 2 yrs & 2 Mo. & 25 days.

[737] Catharine E. Dau. of g. S. & Jane Lafferre Died Mar. 16, 1867 Aged

The grave marker of Lucy, Mrs. Sereno, Wright, Jr.

Charles W. Bryant's notebooks of information on all things to do with early Granville people are treasured possessions of the Granville Historical Society. He carefully recorded the epitaphs from the Old Colony Burying Ground, as in this example.

(All four images)
Granville Historical Society Archives

In 1880 another newspaper appeared on the scene in Granville: *The Granville Times*. It was to run, with a few intermissions, for 60 years, recording the town and township in minute detail.

The Granville Times

OL. XXVII.   GRANVILLE, O., THURSDAY AFTERNOON, AUGUST 3, 1905.   NO. 31

On account of the Centennial The TIMES will be furnished all new subscribers from now until January 1, '06 for 50 cents. This is a great opportunity to secure the local paper for little money and get in touch with the coming Centennial.

GRANVILLE IMPROVEMENTS

Wonderful Activity In Building Line— New Structures Going Up All Over Town.

Few towns in Ohio the size of Granville can boast of the facilities which she possesses. Granville is abreast with the times, possessing electric street railway, excellent telephone service, telegraph, electric lights, natural gas, water works, banking, hotel accommodations, and best of all, one of the best educational centers in the state. There is probably no other town in Ohio the size of Granville that has under construction so as fine buildings as are now going up on the campus grounds of Shepardson College,—the handsome three-story brick dormitory and the new gymnasium building. A large force of men are now employed on these two buildings, and work is being pushed as rapidly as possible.

The foundation dence to be Charles the work on be pushed arrives.

The carp busily enga side finish c sonage, cor way.

The new Dr. A. K. Clouse's L

Work on the new gymnasium for Shepardson College is progressing quite rapidly. The first story, which is of stone, has been completed and the workmen have the second story, which is of brick, nearly completed.

The new residence of Mr. F. H. Buxton on South Pearl street is now being plastered, and it is thought the home will be ready for occupancy by the first of September.

The handsome new residence being erected by Mr. William Jones, just east of the village, on the Granville and Newark road, is now being plastered, and will be ready for occupancy in a short time.

The contractors who are engaged in constructing the new dormitory and gymnasium for Shepardron College also have the contract for finishing the basements of Doane Academy and the east dormitory A large number work on bo fidently ex completed by the time fall.

GAS NOTES.

The Ohio Fuel Supply company drilled in a strong well on the farm of Mr. Richard Purdy near Martinsburg Saturday. A stake has been driven for a second well on that farm.

Hall and McMillen have leased their farm in Union township to the Columbus Natural Gas Co. recently. the rig on the Granby farm has been moved to the Anderson farm. The Simon's rig was moved to the Stone farm, both in Union township.

A two million well came in on the L. N. White farm in Union township belonging to Mr. Heisey on Tuesday evening. The well was tubed in yesterday and the well is perfectly dry. The drillers will go from this well to the Baker farm and the tools will be strung Friday.

ers, who e to the lay pipes he Coun- esday and of town, as Com- is in the field and e The wells is ay. The recently, of them takes the

be Sarah Friday. hen first is now

WERHLE FOUNDRY

Reopened Monday Under Police Protection After Having Been Closed Down One Month.

The big Wehrle Stove Works at Newark, which has been closed down during the past month, and where a number of Granville men are employed, reopened on Monday morning under police protection. Only the polishing department is being operated, and it is understood that this will be continued until the work is cleaned up. The moulders will then be recalled and the factory will resume the former routine.

Among business men and those who have the welfare of the city at heart, the news that the works would be opened was as food to the famished.

Fifty thousand dollars was paid to work week the c sour chan it ext and fore, Th of th those derst the c tion It ninet desig tors, track sible build

LEVI BEVARD.

The Accused Murderer of Mrs. Frances Werts Released on Five Thousand Dollars Bond.

Levi Bevard, the accused murderer of Mrs. Frances Werts, has been released under bond. The arrangements for the release were completed late Saturday afternoon and when the turnkey at the county jail unlocked Bevard's cell and announced that he was released, the big man all but wept with the joy he felt.

Bevard has been confined at the big prison on the canal for just 51 days, having arrived eight days after the cruel murder was committed. His long incarceration in the jail has wrought wonders in the prisoner's personal appearance. Instead of the swarthy complexioned farmer who was in a cornfield, a sunken cheeks teller's office be- Messrs. Smythe

ce to the office Bevard remain- re going home. have worked since he was ad jury. Mayor t the signatures cause with one relatives of the

signers of the hat they were court finally

the bond were wife, Daniel

Judson Evans at the linotype.

Donald W. Young, William H. Kussmaul, owner, and Judson Evans working on *The Granville Times* about 1912. The press was housed upstairs in the building at the northwest corner of Prospect and Broadway.

In 1980 Donald W. Young revisited the equipment still housed on North Prospect Street. Donald began working at the *Times* at age sixteen as an apprentice. He eventually purchased the business.

(Young image) Gloria Hoover, used with permission

(Other images) Granville Historical Society Archives

Francis W. Shepardson, 1862-1937, wrote many short pieces about Granville history which appeared in the *Times*. He was a graduate of Denison University and a professor at the University of Chicago. He also wrote the 1931 Centennial History of Denison University.

The old burying ground so loved by Charles W. Bryant was virtually abandoned when Maple Grove Cemetery opened in 1863, being used occasionally, usually for additional family graves or for infant burials. In 1909 the local chapter of the Daughters of the American Revolution organized a clean-up day. The women enlisted Village officials and male church members to do the hard labor. This photograph of their work day is taken looking from east to west. Notice the telephone poles marching down the center avenue.

In 1923 the ladies joined in the clean-up. Dora Case stands left of center in her hat and pearls. Kate Shepard Hines is seated on the grass next to her. This picture looks east down Maple Street.

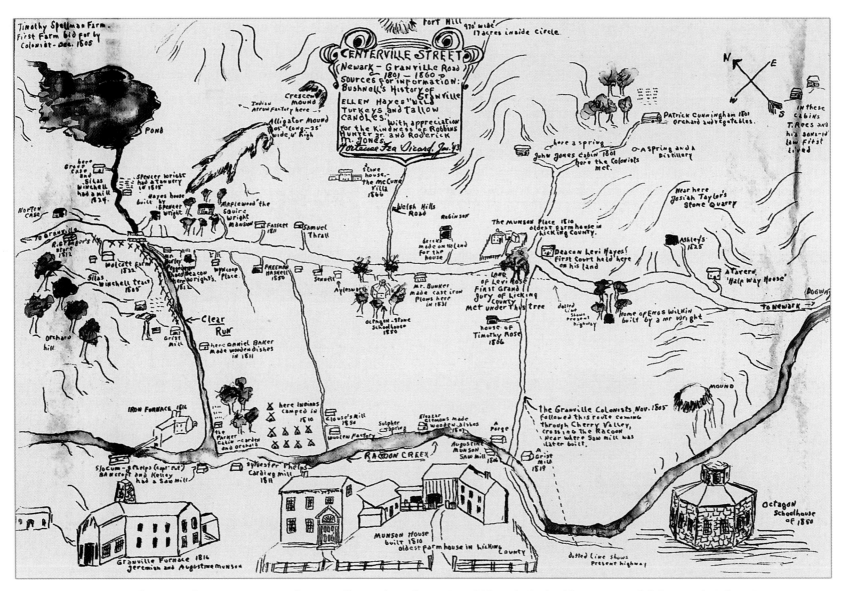

A fanciful depiction of Centerville Street, or Newark-Granville Road, made in 1943. Although the buildings pictured did exist, their locations are somewhat awry, as are the streets and intersections.

Granville Historical Society Archives

Clara Sinnett White, 1862–1947. An accomplished pianist, she sponsored the arts in Granville, and worked tirelessly for the establishment of the Granville Public Library at 217 East Broadway.

(Top three images)
Granville Historical Society Archives

Charles Browne White, 1870-1945, instructor in Latin at Doane Academy, the Denison University prep school, was Granville's "resident intellectual." He married Clara Sinnett in 1900, and the couple lived in Clara's family home on Mt. Parnassus. His essays on Granville history, natural history, and other subjects were collected in the book, *The Philosopher of Mt. Parnassus*, published in 1948.

Photo: Rolan Thompson

While the stone bank building on Broadway was being renovated as the Museum of the Granville Historical Society , William Utter was collecting material for his *Granville, the Story of an Ohio Village*. He and his wife, Alma, traveled to Granville, Massachusetts, at one point. In this photo, Dr. Utter (left) pauses near a covered bridge somewhere in New England. The Utters' traveling companions for this trip were Hubert and Oese Robinson. Hubert is pictured with Dr. Utter.

Granville Life-Style Museum

The Historical Society building, at left, before its 1950s restoration. The building had been built in 1815 as a bank, and had served numerous other uses. Clara White and her husband had been caretakers of the archives and artifacts for many years without a safe place for their storage. She left the funds for the purchase and restoration of the little building by the society on her death in 1947.

William T. Richards (1907–1988), was an engineer by profession, working for many years at Bell Labs. But he was an avid historian of all things having to do with farm machinery. One hot day in 1984 Bill Richards was in an old local barn looking at antique equipment. His picture was taken as he paused to rest.

Gloria Hoover, used with permission

Richard Howe at the popular tool exhibit in the museum's basement. Howe was a photography fan, and collected many of the pictures featured in this volume, usually writing clear descriptions and identifications.

Granville Historical Society Archives

Minnie Hite Moody left Granville as a young newlywed during World War I. She had a career as a novelist and poet while living in Atlanta, Georgia, and summering in Granville with relatives. After many years she returned to live out her life in her beloved Tannery Hill home. She turned to writing newspaper columns, titled "I Remember, I Remember," on her memories of growing up in Granville and of all the personalities of the town.

Granville Historical Society Archives

Horace King, Denison University professor of art, was the spearhead for the naming of many village homes to the National Register of Historic Places. His finely detailed drawings of local buildings were published in *Granville: Massachusetts to Ohio* in 1989.

Denison University Archives

Rolan Thompson, a prolific Granville photographer from 1948 until about 1980, was noted for his portraits and local scenes. Some of his best work was the recording of Denison University theater presentations. Below is a scene from "Bell, Book and Candle" featuring John Davidson, Ann Matesich, and Donald Knight.

(Both images)
Denison University Archives

"Touch of a Poet" was presented at Denison in March of 1972. The set was designed by Calvin Morgan. Pictured here are Vincent McNally and Marjorie MacKinnon, in a photo by Rolan Thompson.

In 1970 the Granville area once again had a newspaper, *The Granville Sentinel*. The paper has undergone several changes of owners and editors, but in 2004 remains the premier source of local news.

Sentinel editor and photographer Charles A. Peterson, photographed in 2004.

Longtime reporter of Granville news, Mary Roberts at her desk before her retirement.

The Granville Sentinel

(The other three images)
Granville Historical Society Archives

Amy Deeds, editor in 2004 of the companion to *The Granville Sentinel, Your Community Booster*.

Successful Granville businessman Alfred Avery built his house in 1842 in the popular Greek Revival style. It remained a private residence until 1903 when, like many of the town's larger homes, it became a fraternity house. In 1956 Newark antiquarian Robbins Hunter, Jr., purchased the property and made it his home and shop. On his death the home became a property of the Licking County Historical Society, which began painstaking restoration.

Photo: Gregory B. Mann

Martha Spelman Downer on her front porch in the late 1800s.

(Left and below)
The Robbins Hunter Museum/Avery Downer House

Robbins Hunter added this "Octagon" to the house.

A historic preservationist analyzes paint samples from one of the rooms of the Avery-Downer House. Meticulous attention to detail is a strong componant of the ongoing restoration.

The Granville Sentinel

In 1869 George Goodrich began construction of this house at 121 South Main, on Sereno Wright's old lot. In 1918 Hubert and Oese Robinson moved into the house, where they lived out their lives. Hubert was the last living member of a long-time Granville family whose possessions, some dating to the early 1800s, eventually were accumulated by Oese. The museum was established according to the provisions of Oese's will as a showcase for the possessions and as an archive of hundreds of letters and photographs.

Granville Historical Society Archives

One of the attractions at the Granville Life-Style Museum is the lovely garden. Here Mary Ellen Everett tends the rose bed.

Director Marilyn Anderson looks on as a group of children learn old-fashioned methods of washing clothing. This photo is from the early 1990s.

(Bottom images left and right)
Granville Life-Style Museum

A small part of the quilt collection displayed on the music room couch.

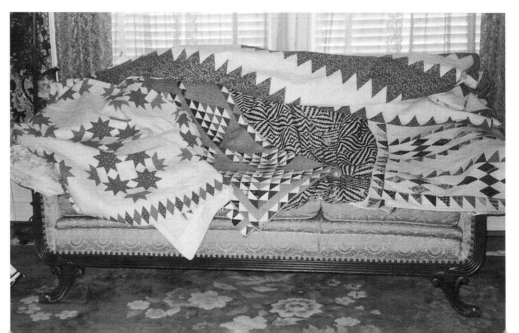

Bill Hoffman and John Senn at one of the volunteer work sessions at Old Colony.

A newly restored area of the cemetery.

By 1990 the old burying ground had once again run to weeds. Tombstones were broken or buried and epitaphs were illegible. A cemetery board was created with the co-operation of the village, township, and Historical Society, and experts were called in to assess the situation. The work of restoration was begun in 1992 under the guidance of professional cemetery restorationists. Workers often relied on the transcribed notes of Charles Webster Bryant.

One evening in late spring of each year, some of Granville's departed citizens live again, chatting with visitors about their lives and adventures. John Senn holds forth in his favorite role: Sereno Wright.

(All four images)
Granville Historical Society Archives

CHAPTER 12

Transitions

Transition, shift, change, growth—words that can encourage or worry, soothe or enrage. But change is a fact of life, and each child born adapts easily to what his parents find strange. Each generation in Granville has lived in an entirely different town from that which older citizens knew, but all the while being Granvillians. Along the way there have been some special changes, pictured in this chapter, some as gradual as the development of a university on a hill, some as quick and startling as the flash of a flame.

(Facing page)
View from the Presbyterian Church toward the west, illustrating the mingling of Denison University, Shepardson College, and the Village, in an era when roads, parking lots, and large trees did not yet dominate the scene.

Granville Historical Society Archives

Even in a seemingly empty space there has often been layer upon layer of change. In 1984 an archaeological dig took place east of the village on what had been part of Bryn Du Farms, and before that the Munson Farm. During the dig, Native-American artifacts were unearthed that dated to the Middle Woodland period, or 100 B.C. to 400 A.D. The flat field shown here, looking south, was also the site of the cabins of the first white settlers in Granville Township. The Munson home and barn are visible on the upper left. Newark-Granville Road runs across the fields from left to right. Route 16 is beyond the first line of trees.

Licking County Archaeological and Landmarks Society

The beautiful valley in 2004. Notice that the gap in the hills for the power line is the same in both this and the photogaph above. New houses have sprung up almost from end to end of the space in just 20 years.

Granville Historical Society Archives

(Photo: William Holloway)

The beginning of construction at Erinwood, at the Munson Farm site. The boulder, later moved a few feet to the east, commemorates the site of the first log cabins in the township, built by settlers who moved on after the company from New England arrived on the scene. Newark-Granville Road, the former Centerville Street, rolls through a broad, flat plain that is ideal for hunting, farming, or building, and has been so used whenever mankind has been in the vicinity.

The Granville Sentinel

A warehouse that stood at the Lancaster Road end of the canal feeder, near the old River Road. See the map on page 13.

(All three images)
Granville Historical Society Archives

Elmer Jones and Charles Gregory fishing in about 1905. They are on the north bank of Raccoon Creek, "across from the slaughterhouse," which would put them somewhere near the 2004 site of Ross' Granville Market parking lot.

RANVILLE, OHIO, THURSDAY, JANUARY 8, 1931

Along The River Road

"The river road will be abandoned soon for a new way built straight west to the Lancaster road."—The Granville Times.

Along the river road!
Through covered bridge with rattling plank,
By towpath on the Raccoon's bank,
Past slaughter house, with odors rank,
The cat tails grew 'mid grasses dank,
Along the river road.

Along the river road
For years the tides of travel flowed;
The swaying oxen, spurred by driver's goad;
The farm teams drawing heavy load;
The motor cars of latest mode,
Along the river road.

Along the river road!
In fancy one may see there still
The wagons moving toward the mill,
Which stood hard by Arbutus Hill,
Or to the Furnace, by the rill,
Along the river road.

Along the river road
The "feeder" came to Granville's door,
Bringing supplies for shop and store,
Or famous village products bore
To distant marts, in days of yore,
Along the river road.

Along the river road
Was much of Granville's story laid.
But now a shorter way is made—
Into the past the faces shade!
Into the haze the memories fade!
Along the river road.

—FRANCIS W. SHEPARDSON.

The original River Road closely followed the south bank of Raccoon Creek on its way out of town, winding east toward Newark. Sometime before 1931, the western end was realigned to come out on Lancaster Road opposite Weaver Drive, thus avoiding the growing gravel pit which became Lake Hudson. Although the way was now safer and smoother for automobile traffic, the older generation of drivers probably missed the scenic route with its memories and associations.

Transitions can have a deeply personal, almost spiritual, meaning. Minnie Hite Moody wrote about her memory of the house on the south east corner of Prospect and Broadway, site of the post office, in 1965:

"Those who have never seen Granville except as it now appears cannot envision the beauty of Mrs. John B. Smith's yard in spring-time. Indeed, there are not many left to recall Mrs. Smith, and as I remember with affection that energetic little lady with the brisk broom and the gorgeous lace curtains, the thought skims through my mind that most of us living at present will be lucky if anyone at all pauses to think of us 50 years from now. Mr. Smith was her second husband. Her first husband, Mr. George H. Bragg, is only a name to me, for he died long before I was born. He was a great lover of flowers, and some of the shrubbery of his planting still survives on the fringes of the post office property. When I was a child, passing Mrs. Smith's house was a delight, because the bulb flowers Mr. Bragg had planted long ago in the yard burst into life every spring until the place was a sight to behold. There was an iron fence around the yard, and just inside it bloomed every possible variety of narcissus in big colorful clumps, so that a child could only stand and clutch the pales of the iron fence and marvel. After Mrs. Smith's property had been sold to the government, Mamma remembered Mr. Bragg's bulbs and, though she was in failing health, hastened to make a deal with Mr. Overturf as local represen-tative of the Post Office Department. The result was that many of the bulbs or their descendents are safe in the ground here at this place where I live. Last spring they kept popping up and I would look at the blossoms and wonder where I had seen them before, but it was inside the iron fence where Mrs. Smith lived, and on either side of the walk leading to her front door. I am grateful to Mamma for having the forethought to look after Mr. Bragg's scilla and grape hyacinths, daffodils and poet's narcissus. For with times changing as fast as they do, it is hard to recall clutching an iron fence with both hands and saying polite things to Mrs. Smith in admiration of the early flowers, and trying to understand what it was she was telling me about spring being eternal."

The Smith house at about the time Minnie Hite Moody remembers it, ca. 1905.
Denison University Archives

Photo: Richard Howe

Mrs. Smith's house as demolition begins in preparation for the post office building, 1936. Part of the iron fence remained on the Prospect Street side.
Granville Historical Society Archives

Denison coeds in their class beanies watch the parade for the town's sesquicentennial in 1955. For over a century, Denison and the various women's schools were part of the patchwork of life in Granville. Students roomed, rented, ate, celebrated, competed, and graduated in the circle of the lives of town residents. By the late twentieth century, however, mingling had become less personal. Students were expected to live on campus, and residents of a now-spread-out village did not so readily take advantage of campus activities.

The Opera House had been the Baptist Church until the summer of 1882 when it was moved across Main Street and enlarged. This great building with the elm tree at the corner dominated downtown for nearly 100 years. It served as town hall and post office, and housed a movie theater, shops, and restaurants at various times.

(Both images)
Granville Historical Society Archives

On a spring night in 1982, the Opera House caught fire and was destroyed.
Only heroic effort by firefighters saved next-door St. Luke's from the flames.

The Opera House bell had been removed for repair before the fire and now serves as a memorial.
The Caron family pauses to reflect on the history of this site in June 2004.
Granville Historical Society Archives

CHAPTER 13

Granville's Future:
Its Children

The faces of Granville's children. The community celebrates its past, looks to the future, and continues to invest in its youth.

Left to right: A young man from the 1860s; Charles Webster Bryant as a lad; Burton Wright about 1857; Alice Sinnett about 1862; a young lady from the early 1860s. *(All images)* Granville Historical Society Archives

Ethel Ramsower in June, 1899

Emily and Margaret Colwell in April of 1899.

Leonard Frederick, photographed in 1899.

(All four images)
Granville Historical Society Archives

Two little girls in about 1918, photographed by Richard Howe.

Bob Evans and Ken Murray at the old club house on the Granville Inn Golf Course, about 1930.

Robert Charles Evans

Lorena McDermott and Florence Hollingworth on Sugar Loaf, April, 1941.

Sidney Hollingworth, courtesy of Florence Hollingworth Wright

Armloads of Hoffmans, about 1961.

Hoffman Family

A birthday party at 415 East Broadway.

Granville Historical Society Archives

Photo: William Holloway

Pam Holloway and Erin Apacki in a church musical, 1983.

A good book, a cozy nook,
and a warm spring day, 1981.

Kristen Drake sips from the fountain, 1975.

The Robert Drake Family

Christmas season 1980
on Beechwood Drive.

(Above and top right)
Photo: T. Overholser

Spring Valley lifeguards, 1990.

Roberts Family, courtesy of Anne Ormond

Samuel and Helen Philipps' children, about 1955: Sylvia, Suzy, Warren, Jennifer, and baby brother Andy.

Jennifer Welsh

Florence Hollingworth and friends are ready to go "Halloweening" in 1948.

Sidney Hollingworth,
courtesy of Florence Hollingworth Wright

Jason Porter entertains at Vacation Bible School, 2004.

Granville Historical Society Archives

DOST THOV LOVE LIFE·THEN DO
NOT SQVANDER TIME·FOR THAT
IS THE STVFF LIFE IS MADE OF·

Rachel Wilson Bain at the
gate to Denison University.

Lance Clarke Family

June, 2004 vacation Bible school
at the Presbyterian Church.

First Presbyterian Church of Granville

ACKNOWLEDGMENTS

Several people involved in producing the three volumes of *Granville, Ohio: A Study in Continuity and Change* have volunteered enormous amounts of time and talent to the project. They begin with Charles J. Stoneburner, who conceived of the idea in the early 1990s. Aware of the high standard set by William T. Utter's sesquicentennial history, *Granville, The Story of an Ohio Village,* several members of the Granville Historical Society began meeting to recruit authors and define a concept in 1995. They were Anthony J. Lisska, Florence W. Hoffman, Margaret E. Brooks, Robert N. Drake, Richard D. Shiels, and then Society President Thomas B. Martin. After six years, Tony Lisska, by now a member of the Bicentennial Commission, gave the project new life. Sherry Beck Paprocki joined the Steering Committee, as did Clarke L. Wilhelm when he agreed to serve as editor of the book of essays. The last to join, Lance L. Clarke, volunteered his services while serving as President Elect of the Granville Historical Society in 2004 and soon had two important advisors from the Battelle Institute, Jean E. Schelhorn and Joseph E. Sheldrick, aboard his new committee. As expertise was needed, he recruited Susan Stoner Leithauser, William E. Holloway, Kenneth C. Apacki, Douglas S. Barno, Lyn Boone, and Charles F. Metzger to constitute his Printing-and-Marketing Committee. Each brought enormous energy and ability to the project. Financial support, so critical at the time for the morale of the Steering Committee, came generously from The Granville Foundation, The Huntington Bank, Denison University, and the Granville Bicentennial Commission. An unnamed guarantor's generosity enabled the project to go forward without cuts in quality in order to meet a reduced budget. Elizabeth Eaton O'Neill's earlier underwriting of *The Granville Times* indexing project, which was brilliantly accomplished by Laura C. Evans, provided a strong basis for research for several authors.

—THOMAS B. MARTIN
Chair of the Bicentennial Publication Committee

The editors of Volume III are greatly indebted to all those mentioned above and to those who loaned or donated photographs for this Volume. In particular we are indebted to: William E. Holloway for his many kindnesses, and for the technical support and instruction that enabled us to scan and transmit all of the photographs and graphics used in this volume; to Denison University and to Denison Archivist Heather Lyle, who gladly made those resources available to us; to Charles A. Peterson, editor of the *Granville Sentinel* who made its photographic records available; and to Florence Hollingworth Wright for generously loaning her father's photographs. We are also grateful to Robert G. Seith and Sherry Paprocki for rigorous proofreading and editing; to Doris J. Porter for her unflagging encouragement; to Duane Dawley for his expert rendering of glass negatives; to Jodi Weaver Chiles for providing a crucial contact; and to Chad Short and the Village Coffee Company for sustaining us.

—THERESA S. OVERHOLSER and FLORENCE W. HOFFMAN
The Granville Historical Society

INDEX

THE GRANVILLE HISTORICAL SOCIETY

Charles Webster Bryant, Crayton Black, and Francis Shepardson chartered the Granville Historical Society on March 9, 1885. Following the 75th anniversary of the community in 1880 they realized that first hand memories of the founding and early days were vanishing. They determined to preserve the history, memorabilia, and artifacts of the pioneer days. Charles W. Bryant with the Reverend Henry Bushnell began work on a history of the community. Bryant was to do the genealogy and Bushnell the history. We are forever in Bryant's debt for genealogical records and his careful documentation of gravestones in the Old Burying Ground in 1886 shortly before his untimely death later that year. Bushnell published the historical section as *The History of Granville, Licking County, Ohio*, in 1889.

Even in Granville's first fifty years there was an interest in its history. The Reverend Jacob Little, a remarkable moral force in the community wrote the first historical record, published in installments. At the Centennial of the Village in 1905, an entire issue of *The Old Northwest Genealogical Quarterly* was devoted to Granville, with topical articles and extensive lists of church members, pupils in schools, and cemetery epitaphs. Ellen Hayes wrote a charming work on the changing world with the transition to artificial light and industrial progress in *Wild Turkeys and Tallow Candles*, published in 1915.

The Sesquicentennial of the Village in 1955 produced a new comprehensive history, *Granville, The Story of an Ohio Village*, by William T. Utter. A very visible and useful legacy of the sesquicentennial is the museum housed in the 1816 building that had been the Bank of the Alexandrian Society. It had later housed shops, restaurants, barbershops, and the interurban station. The possessions of the Society, moved from one storage room to another before being sheltered by Charles B. White and his wife Clara Sinnett White, found a home there. The building also holds the rich archives of the society with records and images of the past two hundred years.

Governed by a Board of managers elected by the membership, the Society publishes a quarterly, *The Historical Times*, presents programs of local historical interest, and in 2000 conducted an oral history project to verbally document the past fifty years. It sponsors a Civil War Roundtable, is parent to the Welsh Cambrian Society, presents an award to the Historian of the Year, and an annual award to a High School student who excels in history. The Society maintains the Museum and the Old Academy Building, built as a school in 1833.

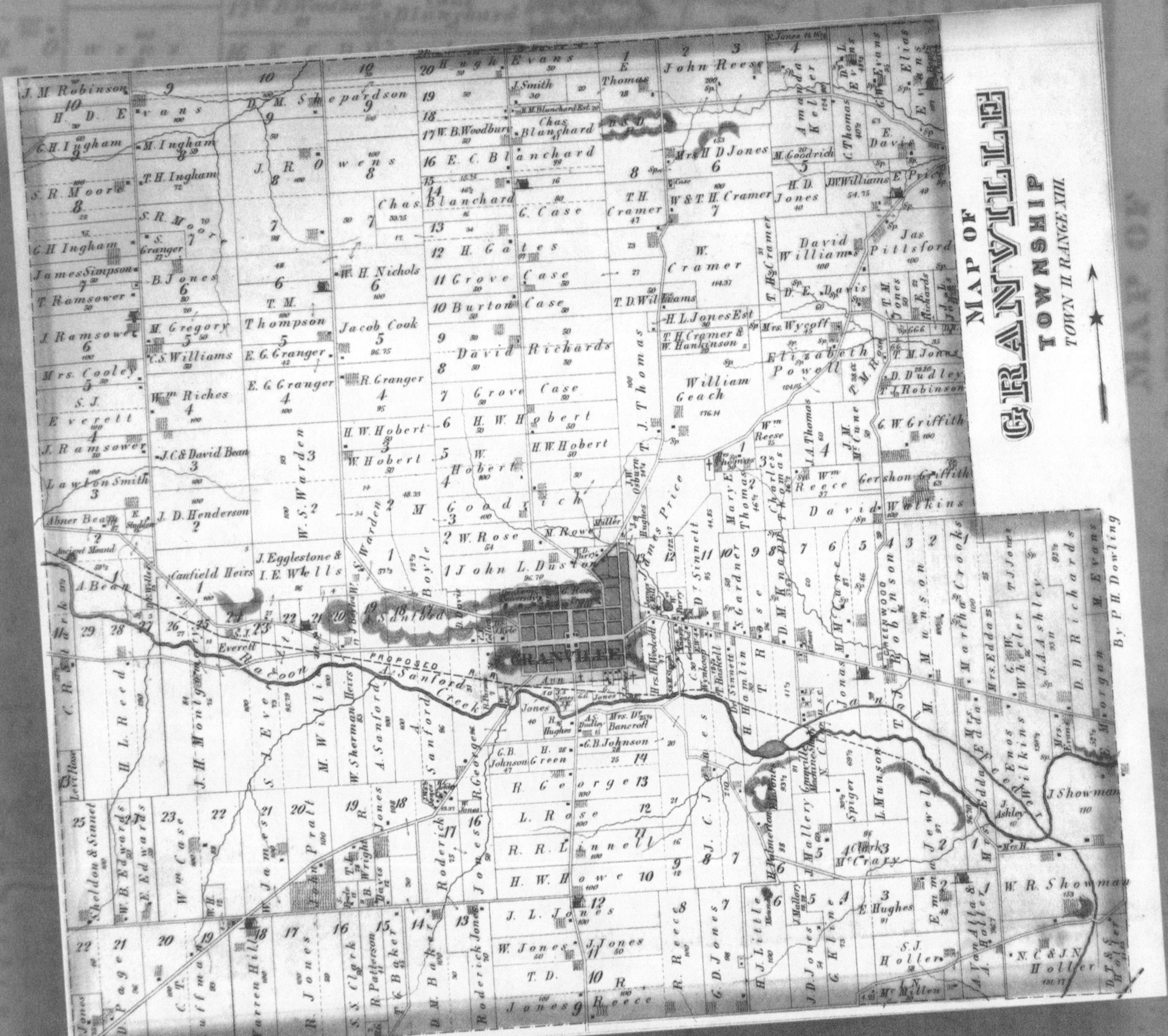

MAP OF
GRANVILLE
TOWNSHIP
TOWN II RANGE XIII.
By P.H. Dowling
GRANVILLE
Raccoon Creek
PROPOSED
J. M. Robinson
H. D. Evans
G. H. Ingham
M. Ingham
S. R. Moore
T. H. Ingham
D. M. Shepardson
J. R. Owens
Hugh Evans
J. Smith
E. Thomas
John Reese
W. B. Woodbury
Chas. Blanchard
E. C. Blanchard
Mrs. H. D. Jones
M. Goodrich
C. Thomas
H. D. Jones
J. W. Williams
W & T. H. Cramer
T. H. Cramer
G. Case
H. Gates
Grove Case
Burton Case
W. H. Nichols
T. M. Thompson
David Williams
Jas. Pittsford
W. Cramer
T. D. Williams
D. E. Davis
H. L. Jones Est
James Simpson
T. Ramsower
B. Jones
J. Ramsower
M. Gregory
C. S. Williams
E. G. Granger
Jacob Cook
R. Granger
David Richards
T. H. Cramer & W. Hankinson
Mrs. Wycoff
Elizabeth Powell
T. M. Jones
D. Dudley
T. J. Robinson
Mrs. Cooley
S. J. Everett
Wm. Riches
William Geach
G. W. Griffith
H. W. Hobert
W. Hobert
J. C. & David Bean
Lawton Smith
J. D. Henderson
Abner Bean
W. S. Warden
M. Goodrich
W. Rose
M. Rowe
Gershon Griffith
David Watkins
Wm. Reese
Mary E. Thomas
Charles Thomas
James Price
J. Egglestone & I. E. Wells
Canfield Heirs
A. Bean
John L. Duston
A. Sanford
Ancient Mound
H. L. Reed
J. H. Montgomery
W. Sherman Heirs
A. Sanford
Jones
A. S. Dudley
Mrs. Dr. Bancroft
G. B. Johnson
H. Green
R. George
L. Rose
R. R. Linnell
H. W. Howe
J. L. Jones
W. Jones
J. Jones
T. D. Jones
R. Reece
R. Reese
G. D. Jones
H. J. Little
J. D. Jones
C. Kline
E. Hughes
S. J. Holler
N. C. & J. N. Holler
W. R. Showman
J. Showman
J. Ashley
J. Munson
Clark McCrary
D. M. Knapp
Sheldon & Sinnet
W. B. Edwards
E. Edwards
Wm. Case
John Pratt
Warren Hill
R. Jones
S. S. Clark
R. Patterson
T. C. Baker
D. M. Baker
Roderick Jones
M. Evans
D. D. Richards
J. A. Ashley
Mrs. Eddas
L. D. Page
C. T. Huffman